# REGINA'S
# INTERNATIONAL
# VEGETARIAN
# FAVORITES

# REGINA'S INTERNATIONAL VEGETARIAN FAVORITES

*Regina Campbell*

HPBOOKS

The recipes in this book are to be followed exactly as written. Neither the author nor the publisher is responsible for your specific health or allergy needs that may require medical supervision, or for any adverse reaction to the recipes contained in this book.

HPBooks
Published by The Berkley Publishing Group
A division of Penguin Group (USA) Inc.
375 Hudson Street
New York, New York 10014

First edition: June 2003

Library of Congress Cataloging-in-Publication Data

Campbell, Regina.
    Regina's international vegetarian favorites / Regina Campbell.— 1st ed.
        p.  cm.
    Includes index.
    ISBN 1-55788-410-2
    1. Vegetarian cookery.   2. Cookery, International.   I. Title.

TX837.C326   2003
641.5'636—dc21
                                                            2002192184

PRINTED IN THE UNITED STATES OF AMERICA

10   9   8   7   6   5   4   3   2   1

*This is dedicated to our elders and our offspring, our brothers and sisters, our friends and acquaintances around the globe who take their places at the daily table in the spirit of sharing their days together with food and love.*

# CONTENTS

# ACKNOWLEDGMENTS

One of the lovely things about the publishing industry is that, through this often-overlooked acknowledgments section, it gives us the opportunity to show our gratitude for all of those who help us along the way in our endeavors.

If it wasn't for the loving and good-natured help of Julie Hawkins, I would not have been able to bring this to you in a sane fashion. It has always been difficult for me to let go of the reins in my career, both in television and with my writing and cooking. But there comes a time when we have to trust that we are indeed replaceable. When keeping control was no longer an option in my life, an angel, my sister, Denise, delivered another angel, Julie, to me. Her creativity and her ability to manifest the visions of others added greatly to the diversity of this cookbook. Our favorite poetess, Viola Weinberg, added historical spice to the presentation, which I know you'll enjoy.

Also, I would like to thank Biba Caggiano, a wonderful author of Italian cookbooks, for sharing her literary agents, Eric and Maureen Lasher, with me. They have been a dream to work with, guiding me through the nuances of a sometimes overwhelmingly confusing industry.

And of course, no cookbook author should overlook the true heroes of the industry, the testers. For good and bad, my son, Stuart, my sister, Denise, and her family, my father and his dear wife, May, my friend Linda Davis Foster, and countless other special men and women in my life have all been willing to take at least one mouthful of my newest creation. Thank all of you for being good sports.

# INTRODUCTION

W hen people ask me what I eat if I don't eat meat, I'm somewhat dumbfounded. Having had the privilege of spending time in the kitchens of some of the greatest chefs and watching one astounding vegetarian creation after another unfold, I've all but forgotten the days when I used to ask *myself* the same question.

All one needs to do is go through the cookbook aisle at any large bookseller to see the vast array of vegetarian cookbooks. There are tens of thousands of original and wonderful-tasting recipes contained within those pages. But one theme I have repeatedly searched for, with little success, has been books that offer full vegetarian menus from around the globe. That is why I decided to put my energies into *Regina's International Vegetarian Favorites,* because, like many cookbook authors, I write as much for myself as anyone else—in part, because it's the only way my recipes will ever stay organized, and because I like my cooking!

So contained within the following pages is a food journey around the world. You'll find appetizers, soups, salads, side dishes, entrées, desserts, and beverages from thirteen regions of the world, from the Mediterranean to the Caribbean Islands to Southeast Asia and many places in between. Many of the dishes are some of the familiar, best-loved recipes you would order from a menu in your favorite ethnic restaurant. Others are creations that include the ingredients commonly used in a particular part of the world but that are put together in an original way. Alongside the recipes are informative stories describing some of the special ingredients and cooking processes used in a given ethnic cuisine, while each recipe is accompanied by an interesting note or background on the dish.

From Vietnamese Salad Rolls to Mu Shu Vegetables to Wild Mushroom Soup with Crème Fraîche, to Onion Tart to Curried Cauliflower Soup to Stuffed Figs in Chocolate with Turkish Coffee, let's go on a pleasure trip through villages and cities around the world and feast at their tables!

# REGINA'S
# INTERNATIONAL
# VEGETARIAN
# FAVORITES

# APPETIZERS
*Just the Beginning . . .*

■ ■ ■

Like the first kiss of a new romance, the appetizer is what warms us to the dining experience that lies ahead. But like all relationships in modern times, the role of the appetizer is changing.

Once upon a time, the appetizer was served strictly as the prelude to a meal. But with the shift in awareness to a diet more lean and light, the appetizer may now show up at any point in the menu. People such as me will often order a couple of appetizers as an entire meal when dining out. This is made more enjoyable by the growing creativity within the world of vegetarian cuisine. This mini-course can range from a simple yet elegant dish of sautéed mushrooms such as my Mushrooms with Golden Tears from Eastern Europe, or a French Onion Tart, or our new twist on an old Middle Eastern favorite, Grilled Eggplant Dip.

I encourage you to use each course as you choose and to adapt the size of the meal to your own body's needs. For me, the appetizer is the most anticipated dish, when the appetite is at its greatest—but then I've always been a fool for the first kiss!

# *Green Onion Pancakes*

*What is simpler than fresh green onions and potatoes flavored by no more than salt and butter? Simple as this recipe is, the delicate flavor of this classic Chinese appetizer carries a homestyle elegance.*

**Preparation Time: 30 minutes ▪ Cooking Time: 10 minutes ▪ Makes 8 pancakes**

▪ ▪ ▪

> 1¼ cups all-purpose flour
>
> 4 teaspoons baking powder
>
> 1 teaspoon salt
>
> 1 cup milk
>
> 2 large eggs, lightly beaten
>
> 5 tablespoons unsalted butter, melted
>
> 1 cup mashed, cooked russet potato (about 1 large potato)
>
> 2 bunches green onions (green and white parts), trimmed and finely chopped

1. Place the flour, baking powder, and salt in a mixing bowl and stir to combine. Add the milk, eggs, butter, mashed potato, and onions. Mix until well blended. If too thick, add more milk.

2. Heat a griddle over medium heat. Brush with oil or butter. For each pancake, ladle ¼ cup batter onto the hot griddle. Cook about 3 minutes, until browned on the bottoms; flip and cook on the other side until golden brown.

# Mushrooms with Golden Tears

*When Garrik Danilov, a Russian friend of mine, told me how delicious this dish was, I reacted less than enthusiastically. "You can make something remarkable with only salt and mushrooms? Show me." It is indeed difficult to imagine such a simple preparation and ingredient list could yield such intensely rich flavors, yet it's true, my friends. The amber-colored liquid that "weeps" into the cap is a mushroom connoisseur's dream. Share them in an intimate setting, as it requires skill to get the mushroom to the mouth with the liquid gold intact.*

**Preparation Time: 10 minutes ▪ Cooking Time: 10 minutes ▪ Makes 4 to 6 servings**

▪ ▪ ▪

> 1 pound fresh mushrooms
> Olive oil
> About ½ teaspoon sea salt

1. Gently brush the mushrooms free of any debris.

2. Gently remove the stems from the mushrooms, making sure not to break the cap.

3. Brush the bottom of a skillet with olive oil. Place the mushrooms, cap side up, in the skillet. Put a light sprinkling of sea salt in the cavity of each mushroom. Turn the heat to medium. Cover the skillet and let the mushrooms cook for 10 minutes. Mushroom juice will form inside the cavities of each mushroom.

4. Carefully remove the mushrooms from the pan with a spoon. Serve hot.

# Piroshkis

*Piroshkis were a favorite of mine before I became a vegetarian, particularly those from my favorite Russian deli in the Avenues in San Francisco. Once I made the break from eating meat, I spent years going without piroshkis. Ultimately, I came up with this earthy and highly flavorful vegetarian piroshki. In addition to containing no meat, it does not require deep-frying, as does the traditional Eastern European version.*

**Preparation Time: 60 minutes ▪ Cooking Time: 30 minutes ▪ Makes 8 portions**

▪ ▪ ▪

1 small onion, diced

2 cups chopped fresh mushrooms

4 cups shredded cabbage or 6 cups chopped spinach

1½ teaspoons balsamic vinegar

½ teaspoon caraway seeds

Salt and freshly ground black pepper, to taste

½ cup water or vegetable broth

1 (10-ounce) can refrigerated biscuit dough, or ¼ recipe dough for Homemade Biscuits (page 7)

¾ cup coarsely grated Gouda or Edam cheese

Olive oil, for brushing

1. Preheat the oven to 400F (205C). Grease a large baking sheet. In a large skillet, cook the onion, mushrooms, cabbage, balsamic vinegar, caraway seeds, salt, and pepper in the water over medium-high heat until softened and liquid has evaporated, about 10 minutes.

2. On a flat work surface, roll each canned biscuit out to a 4- to 5-inch circle. If using the biscuit dough, use about ¼ cup dough for each piroshki and roll out to a 4- to 5-inch circle on a floured work surface. Spoon 3 tablespoons vegetable mixture plus

2 tablespoons cheese onto one half of the dough. Fold the uncovered side of the dough over the top of the vegetable mixture to form a turnover shape. Press the edges together. Brush the top with olive oil. Repeat with remaining biscuits, filling, and cheese.

3. Place the turnovers on a greased baking sheet. Bake for 15 minutes, until golden brown.

# Homemade Biscuits

*This original recipe was called angel biscuits, and heavenly they are! I have included the entire recipe, which I received from my former mother-in-law, Lavonna. It's been in the family for decades, and I cannot see any reason to update what is already perfect. If you like, make half the recipe, use some of the dough for the Piroshkis (page 5), and bake the remaining dough later as biscuits.*

**Preparation Time: 20 minutes ▪ Cooking Time: 15 minutes ▪ Makes 24 biscuits**

▪ ▪ ▪

> 5 cups all-purpose flour
> 1 teaspoon baking powder
> 1 teaspoon baking soda
> 1 teaspoon salt
> 3 tablespoons sugar
> ¾ cup (12 tablespoons) unsalted butter
> 2 cups buttermilk
> 1 package active dry yeast dissolved in ½ cup lukewarm water

1. Preheat the oven to 400F (205C). Grease a large baking sheet. Sift together the flour, baking powder, baking soda, salt, and sugar. Cut in the butter with two knives. Add the buttermilk and dissolved yeast. Mix with a spoon until all the flour is moistened. Cover the bowl and place in the refrigerator until ready to use. (It will last for a few days.)

2. Roll the dough out on a floured board to ½-inch thickness. Cut the biscuits with a biscuit cutter or upside-down glass. Place the biscuits on the prepared baking sheet. Bake for 12 to 15 minutes until golden brown.

# Leek and Cheese Pockets

*The perfect accompaniment to a glass of champagne, these little pastry "purses" offer a rich flavor from the pungent Old Amsterdam cheese along with a light, flaky texture. Any sharp white cheese will do if you can't find Old Amsterdam.*

**Preparation Time: 45 minutes • Cooking Time: 10 minutes • Makes about 16 pockets**

■ ■ ■

> 3 medium leeks, white parts only, cut into ¼-inch pieces
> 1 tablespoon unsalted butter
> Salt and white pepper, to taste
> Nutmeg, preferably freshly grated, to taste
> 12 sheets phyllo dough
> 3 tablespoons unsalted butter, melted
> ¾ cup grated cheese such as Old Amsterdam, Asiago, aged Gouda,
>    Bel Paese, or Gruyère

1. Preheat the oven to 375F (190C). Line a baking sheet with parchment paper. Cook the leeks in the 1 tablespoon butter in a small skillet over medium-high heat until the leeks are softened. Season with salt, white pepper, and nutmeg. Remove from the heat and set aside.

2. On a work surface, lay out the phyllo. Place 4 phyllo sheets on top of each other, brushing each phyllo sheet with butter. Cut the phyllo into 5- to 6-inch squares. (Keep remaining phyllo covered.)

3. Place 2 teaspoons leeks and 2 teaspoons cheese on each phyllo square.

4. Pull up all four corners into the center and twist the edges all together. Repeat with remaining leeks, cheese, and phyllo.

5. Place the pockets on the prepared baking sheet and bake for 8 to 10 minutes, until golden.

# Onion Tart

*The beauty of this little tart is that it has only one-third the fat from cream that classic French quiches have. Done more in the style of an Italian* torta, *it uses just enough dairy to create a smooth and rich texture. Balsamic vinegar and the sharpness of the cheese give a big lift to the flavor of this onion tart, which can be served as a first course or as a luncheon entrée.*

**Preparation Time: 45 minutes** ▪ **Cooking Time: 30 minutes** ▪ **Makes 6 servings**

9-inch purchased pie crust, or make
according to recipe (page 201)

3½ cups thinly sliced yellow onions

1 tablespoon balsamic vinegar

½ cup vegetable broth

Salt, to taste

¾ cup coarsely grated hard cheese,
such as Reggiano, Asiago, or
Grana Padano

4 eggs

½ cup half-and-half

White pepper

1. Preheat the oven to 400F (205C). Line the pie crust with foil and weight it down with a few dry beans. Bake the pie crust for 5 minutes. Remove from the oven and set aside. Decrease oven temperature to 375F (190C).

2. Cook the onions, balsamic vinegar, vegetable broth, and salt in a medium skillet over medium-high heat until the onions are softened.

3. Spoon the onion mixture evenly into the prebaked pie shell.

4. Sprinkle the cheese over the onion mixture.

5. In a mixing bowl, beat the eggs lightly. Add the half-and-half and white pepper. Mix well.

6. Gently pour the egg mixture on top of the onion mixture.

7. Bake for 30 minutes, until the crust is golden in color and the filling is firmly set.

# Pastis: More Than a Liqueur

Drinking pastis on a sunny afternoon over a game of *boules* or over the day's gossip with a friend is a pastime in France. The first time I was exposed to this anise-flavored drink was at the Gare de Lyon train station in Paris. I spotted this elegantly turned-out young woman in the true French style—smooth, short hair, little makeup, beautifully cut taupe-colored suit with feminine lines, and no jewelry. She was accompanied by an elegant gentleman who was considerably older than she. I immediately began to imagine scenarios as to whether they were married, having an affair, and so on. But what caught my curiosity even more was this strange drink before them. A small glass decanter arrived along with a bottle of water and two glasses of ice. The clear liqueur was poured first, then the water. The instant the water hit the liqueur, the mixture turned an opaque milky color. I immediately asked a French friend to tell me more about this drink, which is called pastis. (The word *pastis* is from an old southern French dialect that means "muddled" or "unclear.")

We drank pastis virtually every afternoon during our stay, which made for lively games of *boules* (the French version of *bocchi* ball). When I returned home I began to learn that pastis is also a wonderful flavor enhancer in sauces, soups, and even desserts. Its licorice flavor is combined with other herbal ingredients, making each producer's pastis slightly different. The two most commonly known pastis are Pernod, which is produced in northern France, and Ricard, made in the south.

I find pastis a more refreshing drink than many of the other anisette liqueurs, as, due to the dilution with water, it is not too sweet. It does, however, conjure up sweet memories.

# Dolmades

Dolmades are surprisingly simple to make, drenched with sun-ripened flavors, and always a delight to dinner guests. In addition to the pleasure they give the palate, they are one of the more nutritious appetizers you'll find. The only tricky part to making dolmades is locating grape leaves. You can usually buy them in a can or jar in specialty food shops or ethnic food stores.

**Preparation Time: 30 minutes ▪ Cooking Time: 30 minutes ▪ Makes 16 to 18 pieces**

▪ ▪ ▪

2 cups vegetable broth

2 tablespoons extra-virgin olive oil

Salt, to taste

1 cup white rice

1/3 cup sun-dried tomatoes, finely minced

1/3 cup kalamata olives, pitted

1/3 cup finely chopped chives

Juice of 1/2 lemon

1 tablespoon balsamic vinegar

Salt and freshly ground black pepper, to taste (go lightly on the salt—there's salt in the cured grape leaves)

1 (16-ounce [dry weight]) jar grape leaves, drained

1. In a saucepan, place the broth, oil, salt, and rice. Bring to a boil, reduce heat to low, and cook for 15 minutes, until the rice is almost done, adding more water if the rice is too firm. Stir in the sun-dried tomatoes and finish cooking rice to the desired texture.

2. Remove from the heat. Add the olives, chives, lemon juice, vinegar, salt, and pepper. Mix gently and allow to cool.

3. Soak the grape leaves in a bowl of warm water for at least 30 minutes, then pat them dry. Place 1 tablespoon rice mixture at the stem end of a grape leaf. Fold in each side, then roll up to make a neat package. Place the filled, rolled leaf on a tray and repeat until all the rice is used. Serve at room temperature or refrigerate until serving.

**Note:** The traditional method of making dolmades requires you to bake the rolls for a time in a baking dish with a small amount of liquid in the bottom, which also softens the rice. I enjoy them the quick and easy way, because the leaves have a little more texture and color.

# Hummus

*This popular Middle Eastern appetizer has begun to appear on a broad variety of menus across the country from delis to elegant cafés and restaurants. Equally as varied are the spicing options for what is basically a bean dip. In this recipe we are staying with a traditional presentation, which reflects the primary flavors of the region—tahini, garlic, and lemon juice. We do, however, give the option of using either the classic garbanzo bean or Italian cannellini bean, which has an exceptionally creamy texture.*

**Preparation Time: 10 minutes ▪ Cooking Time: 0 ▪ Makes 2 cups**

▪ ▪ ▪

1 (16-ounce) can cannellini or garbanzo beans,
  drained
⅓ cup tahini paste
5 tablespoons fresh lemon juice
3 tablespoons extra-virgin olive oil
3 cloves garlic, minced
Pinch of cayenne pepper, or to taste
½ teaspoon ground cumin
Salt, to taste

**TO SERVE:**
Toasted pita bread triangles or pita halves,
  tomato, cucumber, and avocado

1. Place the beans, tahini paste, lemon juice, olive oil, garlic, cayenne pepper, cumin, and salt in a blender or food processor. Process until smooth.

## Tahini Paste

Tahini is an all-natural creamy puree of sesame seeds. As with all nut butters, tahini is high in fat, containing 100 calories per tablespoon. To its credit, however, sesame tahini is very high in calcium, potassium, magnesium, vitamin A, as well as protein. Tahini is normally used in small amounts as a flavor enhancer, adding a rich, nutty flavor to Middle Eastern dishes.

2.  Serve with pita triangles as a dip, or stuff into pita halves with tomato, cucumber, and avocado slices.

**Variation:** Pureed roasted red peppers can be added to the recipe for a fresh twist in flavor as well as adding an attractive pink color to the dish.

# SAMOSAS...

## Baked Samosas

*This popular potato-filled spicy pastry is one of my all-time favorite appetizers, particularly if you bring along a hearty appetite. One of the best features of my version of samosa is that it is baked, not deep-fried.*

**Preparation Time: 1 hour** ▪ **Cooking Time: 20 minutes** ▪ **Makes 12 to 16 pieces**

▪ ▪ ▪

**FILLING**

1½ cups chopped onions

1 to 1½ cups vegetable broth or water

3 russet potatoes, diced into small cubes

3 cloves garlic, minced

¾ teaspoon turmeric

1½ teaspoons Garam Masala (page 120), or purchased

¾ teaspoon salt

⅛ teaspoon cayenne pepper, or to taste

2 tablespoons plus 1 teaspoon fresh lemon juice

1½ cups frozen or fresh green peas

**SOUR CREAM CRUST**

2 cups all-purpose flour

½ teaspoon salt

¾ cup (12 tablespoons) salted butter, chilled

8 ounces (1 cup) sour cream

4 tablespoons cold milk

1. To make the filling: In a large saucepan, add all the filling ingredients except the peas. Cook over low heat, adding small amounts of water if necessary to keep it from

becoming too dry, for about 25 minutes, until the potatoes are tender and the liquid is almost evaporated.

2. Add the peas and cook for 1 to 2 minutes. Set aside.

3. To make the crust: Place the flour and salt in a bowl. Cut the butter into cubes and drop them into the flour. Cut in the butter with two knives until the butter is the size of peas. Quickly add the sour cream and milk and mix gently, taking care not to over-mix. Turn the dough out onto a floured board. Cut the dough into two pieces. Wrap one half and refrigerate it until needed.

4. Preheat the oven to 400F (205C). Lightly grease a large baking sheet. Roll out the dough into a 12-inch square about ¼ inch thick. Cut it into four (6-inch) squares. Spoon a heaping tablespoon of the potato mixture into the center of each square. Fold the corners of the dough up toward the top and press the edges together to seal in the form of a pouch. Repeat with remaining dough and filling.

5. Place the pouches on prepared baking sheet. Bake for 15 to 20 minutes, or until golden brown. Cut the pouches in half and serve hot.

■ ■ ■

# *Tomato Torta*

*One of my favorite foods is a well-made vegetable torta or quiche. The combination of a good flaky crust, quality eggs, tomatoes, and the rich, sharp flavor of a good Parmesan-type cheese make this torta one of the best I've ever experienced (if I do say so myself!).*

**Preparation Time: 30 minutes ▪ Cooking Time: 25 minutes ▪ Makes 6 to 8 servings**

■ ■ ■

> 9-inch purchased pie crust, or make according to recipe (page 201)
> 14½-ounce can chopped tomatoes, or 3 fresh tomatoes, chopped
> ½ cup finely chopped onion
> ½ cup vegetable broth
> 2 tablespoons extra-virgin olive oil (optional)
> ½ cup finely chopped roasted red bell pepper (see page 87)
> 1 tablespoon balsamic vinegar
> ¼ teaspoon salt
> Freshly ground black pepper
> 4 eggs, lightly beaten, or 1 cup egg substitute
> 3 ounces (about 1 cup) grated hard cheese, such as Parmesan,
>    Grana Padano, or aged Asiago

1. Preheat the oven to 400F (205C). Line the uncooked pie crust with foil and weight it down with a few dry beans. Bake the pie crust for 5 minutes. Remove from the oven and set aside. Reduce the oven heat to 375F (190C).

2. In a saucepan, cook the tomatoes, onion, broth, oil, roasted red bell pepper, vinegar, salt, and black pepper over medium heat until the mixture is reduced to a thick and rich-tasting paste with no moisture remaining.

3. Spoon the tomato mixture into the pie shell. Pour the beaten eggs over the tomato mixture. Sprinkle ⅔ cup cheese on top of the tomato mixture and gently stir with the

tines of a fork or your finger to make certain all the ingredients are evenly distributed in the pie shell.

4. Sprinkle the remaining cheese over the top of the filling. Bake for 20 to 25 minutes, until golden on top and firmly set. Serve hot or at room temperature.

## Balsamic Vinegar

The rich, sweet, dark-flavored vinegar known as balsamic has taken the United States by storm. Only a few years ago, many home chefs had never even heard of this variety of vinegar. Today, you can find it in gourmet shops and supermarkets alike, but the product you take home may vary wildly.

The real deal is called *aceto balsammico tradizionale* and is produced in the Modena and Reggio-Emilia provinces of Italy. This is the finest balsamic vinegar available, which is reflected in the price. Why is the vinegar so costly?

The vinegar is made with the grape skins and pulp and taken through an aging process that requires a progression of wooden barrels. As time passes, the liquid evaporates and a syrupy, sweet, mellow vinegar remains. This takes an average of twelve years and can be extended up to twenty-five years and beyond. While visiting the kitchen of Chef Alex Monteil, I was offered a tiny spoonful of twenty-five-year-old balsamic—my first. The richness and depth of flavor was magnificent. He was using it to create a fresh beet juice sorbet, which was unexpectedly bright and flavorful. He credited it to using only the finest balsamic.

The balsamic more commonly found on store shelves for just a few dollars is often a knockoff, a simple wine vinegar spiked with caramel flavoring and coloring. This may work well for many recipes, so I am not discouraging its use. It's worth the money, however, to invest in one good bottle to use sparingly for those special dishes in which you want the balsamic to shine.

# Grilled Eggplant and Onion Bruschetta

*One of the most popular starters at an Italian table is bruschetta. Originally, the dish was created to use up stale bread. Once drizzled with olive oil, rubbed with garlic, and baked, you'd never know this delectable treat was just a resourceful use of old bread. Here we've created a heartier version of bruschetta by incorporating grilled eggplant and onion, rather than the traditional fresh tomato and olive oil.*

**Preparation Time: 1 hour • Cooking Time: 30 minutes • Makes 12 to 14 servings**

■ ■ ■

1 medium globe eggplant

Salt

1 large sweet onion, such as
    Torpedo, Maui, or Vidalia

Extra-virgin olive oil

Balsamic vinegar

Freshly ground black pepper, to
    taste

1½ tablespoons capers,
    drained

**CROSTINI**
1 baguette (day-old is fine)

Extra-virgin olive oil

2 to 3 garlic cloves, crushed

Parsley sprigs

1. Peel and slice the eggplant into ½-inch-thick slices. Place them on a flat work surface, salt the eggplant slices generously, and set aside.

2. Peel and slice the onion into ⅓-inch-thick slices. Place the onion rounds on a grill and cook over medium-high heat until black stripes appear. Turn the onion over and grill on the other side. Remove the onion from the grill and place it in a bowl. Drizzle the onion with a little olive oil; cover and set aside.

3. Rinse the beads of moisture and salt off the eggplant and pat dry with a paper towel. Brush each slice with a little olive oil to keep the eggplant from sticking to the grill. Cook on the grill until the eggplant is softened and black stripes appear. Turn the eggplant and grill on the other side. Place the eggplant into the bowl with the onion.

Drizzle with a little balsamic vinegar and season with salt and pepper; cover and let sit for 30 minutes.

4. Add the capers to the onion and eggplant. Place all the vegetables in a food processor and pulse quickly, 10 to 12 times, until the mixture is coarsely chopped.

5. To make the Crostini: Preheat the oven to 400F (205C). Slice the baguette into ½-inch-thick slices. Brush each slice lightly with olive oil on both sides.

6. Rub each piece of bread with garlic. Place the slices on a baking sheet. Bake for 5 to 7 minutes, until firm. Remove from the oven and allow to cool.

7. Spoon the eggplant mixture on top of each crostini round. Top with a sprig of parsley and serve.

## Tips on Garlic

The truth is, many of us are afraid of garlic. Because it is so pungent to the nose, we tend to back off a bit when including it in recipes. This is a mistake. Having had the good fortune of spending time in the kitchens of many top-flight chefs, one thing is consistent: they seldom hold back on the garlic.

First, only use the freshest garlic available. When purchasing garlic, it should feel firm when pressed. If it gives way under pressure, it's past its prime. Second, never buy it if it has begun to develop little green sprouts, because the green part is bitter.

If you're making a salad or dressing with garlic, pressed garlic is good because the juices will give an aromatic punch to the dish. If you are cooking with garlic, chopped or sliced garlic is better, because the juice is not lost and the garlic retains more of its flavor. Garlic cooks very quickly; do not overcook it. The more you cook garlic, the milder it becomes.

For a very smooth, mild garlic flavor, cut off the top of the head of garlic, exposing the pulp of the cloves. Drizzle a little olive oil on top and bake at 350F (180C) for about 40 minutes. This will give you a soft texture and very mild flavor that can be used at the base of soups, sauces, and a variety of appetizers.

# avocado...
## Avocado Sushi

*As a vegetarian, it can be a little disappointing to accompany your friends to a Japanese restaurant and see the astounding array of sushi available. Nonetheless, it's still worth it to enjoy the one vegetarian sushi on the menu, which is often Avocado Sushi. Don't be intimidated about rolling the sushi; all it requires is an inexpensive sushi rolling mat. The rolling is actually good fun.*

**Preparation Time: 45 minutes ▪ Cooking Time: 0 ▪ Makes 15 to 18 pieces; 4 servings**

▪ ▪ ▪

Japanese Rice (page 130)
2 to 3 tablespoons seasoned rice vinegar
3 toasted nori sheets (dried seaweed)
1 avocado, thinly sliced
1 cucumber, peeled, halved lengthwise, seeded, and cut into ¼–inch julienne strips
Gingered Dipping Sauce (page 22)
Pickled ginger (optional)
Wasabi paste (optional)

1. Prepare the Japanese Rice. Set aside to cool.

2. Add the rice vinegar to the rice and mix thoroughly with your hands.

3. Place a sushi mat on a work surface. Place a sheet of nori on the mat in front of you, with the nori pulled toward the edge of the mat closest to you. Dip your fingers in cold water and take one-third of the rice and pat it firmly onto the closest edge of the seaweed toward the opposite edge, leaving one-third of the farthest edge empty.

4. Place one-third of the avocado and cucumber strips into the center of the rice and begin to roll, firmly, tucking the rolled edge in along the way. Wet the empty end of the nori with water and roll to the end, using even pressure. Repeat with remaining rice, avocado, cucumber, and nori to make three rolls.

5. Cut the rolls into pieces with a sharp, lightly serrated knife. Serve with dipping sauce, ginger, and wasabi (if using).

## ■ *Gingered Dipping Sauce*

**Preparation time: 5 minutes** ▪ **Cooking Time: 0** ▪ **Makes ⅓ cup**

> ¼ cup soy sauce
> 1 tablespoon grated fresh ginger
> 2 tablespoons seasoned rice vinegar
> 8 to 10 drops chili oil
> 8 to 10 drops sesame oil

1. Place the soy sauce in a small bowl.

2. Place the grated ginger into a cheesecloth or a tiny strainer and press to release the ginger juice into the soy sauce. Add the rice vinegar, chili oil, and sesame oil and stir. Store, covered, in the refrigerator for up to 2 weeks.

# Gyozo

*I love pot stickers and was quite disappointed to leave them behind when I first became vegetarian. But there's nothing like desire to ignite the imagination. Mushrooms, garlic, ginger, green onions, and smoked tofu make what I think is a wonderful vegetarian version of pot stickers.*

**Preparation Time: I hour ▪ Cooking Time: I 5 minutes ▪ Makes 24**

■ ■ ■

> 1½ tablespoons peanut oil, plus extra to cook the pot stickers
>
> 5 to 6 (1-inch-long) thin slices fresh ginger
>
> 8 ounces fresh mushrooms, finely minced
>
> 2 green onions (green and white parts), finely sliced
>
> 2 cloves garlic, minced
>
> ⅔ cup shredded carrot
>
> 4 ounces smoked tofu, finely crumbled
>
> 1½ teaspoons shoyu sauce
>
> 48 wonton wrappers
>
> Gingered Dipping Sauce (page 22)

1. In a medium skillet, cook the oil and ginger over medium-high heat for 1 minute. Add the mushrooms, onions, and garlic. When the mushrooms begin to "sweat" out beads of moisture, add the carrot. Cook for 1 minute.

2. Add the tofu and shoyu sauce. Cook for 30 seconds and remove from heat. Transfer to a bowl and let it cool. Remove and discard the ginger.

3. Place the wonton wrappers on a work surface. Place a spoonful of the filling into the center of a wrapper, leaving room around the edge to seal. Dampen the edges of the wrapper using your fingers and a little water. Place another wrapper on top and press them together firmly, taking care not to nick the skin of the wrappers. Repeat with remaining filling and wrappers.

4. Brush the bottom of a large skillet with oil and heat over medium heat. Place the pot stickers in the skillet (cook in batches if needed) and pour in a little water or vegetable broth to allow for steaming. Cover and cook for 2 to 3 minutes, turning once, until golden brown on both sides.

5. Serve hot with the Gingered Dipping Sauce.

# Papaya and Roasted Pepper Salsa

*I love the contrast of sweet, cool papaya and the earthy, smoky flavor of the peppers in this tantalizing salsa recipe. Take the time to read about smoking tomatoes (page 26), as this technique applies not only to this recipe but to others in the book as well. You might also want to read up on roasting peppers (page 87).*

**Preparation Time: 30 minutes ▪ Cooking Time: 15 minutes ▪ Makes 2 cups**

▪ ▪ ▪

2 smoked or grilled tomatoes, peeled, seeded, and chopped (page 26)

2 red bell peppers, roasted, peeled, seeded, and chopped (page 87)

1 roasted chili pepper, peeled, seeded, and chopped (page 87)

½ cup small fresh papaya cubes

Juice of 1 lime

4 tablespoons extra-virgin olive oil

½ cup chopped fresh cilantro

1 tablespoon minced garlic

Salt, to taste

Cayenne pepper, to taste (optional)

1. Mix all the ingredients together in a bowl.

2. Serve as a dip or as a condiment to accompany a main dish.

# Smoking Tomatoes

*Smoked tomatoes are one of the most wonderful concepts I've learned in recent years. You can take an otherwise ordinary dish and infuse it with something special by following a very simple set of instructions. The wonderful part is that you don't need to invest a lot of money for the smoking process. The following are the items you will need. Keep in mind, however, you can buy stovetop smoking kits at many kitchenware shops:*

■ ■ ■

    **An old, large pot with a lid★**
    **Aluminum foil**
    **Mesquite chips**
    **A small grate of some kind★★**
    **Fresh tomatoes**

Line the bottom of your pot, and up the sides at bit, with aluminum foil. Place your mesquite chips in some water for a moment and then remove. Put the chips in the bottom of the pot on the foil. Place a grate above the chips. And, finally, place your tomatoes on top of the grate. Cover the pot with the lid and turn the burner on to medium or medium-high. The mesquite begins producing smoke fairly quickly. Once the smoking process begins, allow it to continue to smoke for at least 10 minutes to get a good strong flavor.

If you want to experiment further with smoked foods, try apples. Smoked apples are a wonderful addition to salads and tarts.

---

★The reason I suggest an old pot is because the smoke can discolor new stainless steel, leaving it with a golden tint.

★★You can use any metal object that can be heated and has ventilation to raise the vegetables or fruit off the mesquite chips. I have used a stainless steel wire soap holder in the past.

# Zucchini and Caramelized-Onion Quesadillas

*I love quesadillas, but all too often, what passes for a quesadilla in Mexican restaurants is a tortilla filled with Cheddar cheese. We are going to take a more creative route here and incorporate not only some additional flavor, but also texture and nutrition by adding grilled zucchini and onions.*

**Preparation Time: 30 minutes ▪ Cooking Time: 5 minutes ▪ Makes 8 servings**

▪ ▪ ▪

1 pound zucchini, sliced crosswise into 4-inch sections, then lengthwise into rectangular-shaped pieces

2 cups thinly sliced onions

½ cup water

¼ teaspoon freshly grated nutmeg

Salt and freshly ground black pepper, to taste

12 flour tortillas

1 cup grated Monterey Jack cheese, or a thinly sliced aged Mexican queso

1 cup grated Cheddar cheese

1. Lightly brush zucchini with oil and place on the grill, cooking both sides until dark stripes appear on the zucchini. Remove from grill and set aside.

2. In a medium skillet, cook the onions and water over medium-high heat until the water evaporates and the onions are translucent. Continue to cook until the onions caramelize. Add the nutmeg, salt, and pepper.

3. Lay a tortilla out flat in a nonstick frying pan or on a griddle. Sprinkle one-sixth of each cheese and onions over the tortilla. Evenly distribute one-sixth of the zucchini slices over the tortilla. Cover the tortilla with another tortilla and cook over medium-low heat until the cheese is melted inside, about 3 to 4 minutes on each side, and quesadillas are golden brown. Repeat with remaining tortillas, onions, zucchini, and cheese.

4. Cut each quesadilla into quarters and serve hot.

# Lavosh Roll-Ups

*This is a very simple but tasty appetizer to serve with any menu. The following ingredients make one roll-up each. Adjust amounts according to how many you would like to make. Each roll-up will yield 6 to 8 appetizer-size pieces.*

**Preparation Time: 30 minutes ▪ Cooking Time: 10 minutes ▪ Makes 6 to 8 appetizer portions**

▪ ▪ ▪

4 ounces mushrooms, finely diced
½ cup water
Generous splash of balsamic vinegar
Pinch turmeric
Seasoning salt, to taste
1 (about 12 × 9-inch) soft lavosh (flat bread), or 1 burrito-size flour tortilla
¼ recipe Herbed Yogurt Cheese (page 30), or ¼ cup crumbled French feta cheese
¼ cup finely chopped red bell pepper

1. In a medium skillet, cook the mushrooms, water, balsamic vinegar, and turmeric over medium-high heat until the moisture has evaporated. Season with seasoning salt. Allow the mixture to cool.

2. Place the lavosh on a flat work surface. Spread a thin layer of the cheese on the bread.

3. Spoon the mushrooms evenly over the cheese.

4. Sprinkle the bell pepper over the mushrooms.

5. Roll the lavosh up like a jelly roll and cut it into 1-inch sections.

6. Serve immediately, because the flatbread dries out quickly. You can wrap it in plastic wrap for a short time before serving, but if allowed to stand too long, the vegetables will make the flatbread too moist.

**Note:** It is important to cook the mushrooms until the moisture is completely gone, or the rolled lavosh will become soggy. If French feta cheese is not available, mix another variety of feta with a little cream cheese to cut the strong, salty flavor.

# Herbed Yogurt Cheese

*Yogurt cheese is lower in fat than many other cheeses and offers friendly yogurt cultures as well. The mild-flavored cheese can be used as a spread with any kind of flavoring.*

**Preparation Time: 15 minutes (plus overnight in refrigerator)** ▪ **Cooking Time: 0** ▪ **Makes 1 cup**

▪ ▪ ▪

> **2 cups plain yogurt**
> **2 to 3 teaspoons chopped fresh herbs such as parsley, dill, basil, or chives**
> **Salt, to taste**

1. Line a strainer with cheesecloth. Put the strainer inside a bowl or pot to catch the liquids. Pour the yogurt into the cheesecloth.

2. Place the strainer and bowl, loosely covered, in the refrigerator and allow it to drain overnight.

3. Turn the yogurt out of the cheesecloth into a small mixing bowl. Stir in the herbs and salt. Place the cheese in an airtight container and refrigerate for up to 1 week.

## *Baba Ghanoush*

*Some dishes are difficult to improve on, so I am not going to try. This simple, classic, Middle Eastern appetizer was featured in my first cookbook, Regina's Vegetarian Table (Prima Publishing, 1998), and was so popular at social gatherings that I decided to share it again. Enjoy it with flatbread, sesame crackers, or seeded lavosh crackers.*

**Preparation Time: 30 minutes ▪ Cooking Time: 1 hour ▪ Makes 2 cups**

▪ ▪ ▪

1 large globe eggplant, about 1½ pounds
2 tablespoons fresh lemon juice
½ teaspoon salt
¼ cup tahini paste
1 teaspoon freshly ground cumin powder
2 cloves garlic, finely minced

1. Place the whole eggplant on a baking sheet. Bake at 350F (180C) for 1 hour, or until softened. Remove from the oven and allow to cool.

2. Peel the skin off of the eggplant with your fingers (the skin should come off easily). Cut the eggplant into a few large pieces and place it in a food processor. Process it until the eggplant is moderately smooth. If you do not use a food processor, mash the eggplant well with a fork.

3. Add the remaining ingredients and mix well.

4. Serve at room temperature as a dip for fresh vegetables or spread inside pita bread.

**Note:** The dip can be stored in the refrigerator in an airtight container for several days.

# *rolls*

## *Vietnamese Salad Rolls*

*Each Southeast Asian restaurant has its own version of salad or spring rolls. However, the best, bar none, is the following recipe, which was given to me by Mai Pham, author of* The Best of Vietnamese and Thai Cooking *(Prima Publishing, 1996) and chef/owner of Lemon Grass. When I'm in a hurry, I have been known to call ahead, swoop in, and carry out these light, crunchy, and incredibly tasty rolls for a quick meal. Such was this infatuation that I invited Mai to join me as a guest on my television program to share this recipe.*

**Preparation Time: 1 hour ▪ Cooking Time: 15 minutes ▪ Makes 8 rolls**

**FILLING**
8 ounces mushrooms, chopped
1 tablespoon extra-virgin olive oil
2 tablespoons water
1 tablespoon hoisin sauce
Salt, to taste
3 ounces rice vermicelli
8 sheets round rice paper
1 cup grated carrots
Several leaves of green leaf lettuce
Fresh mint
1 cup fresh bean sprouts

**DIPPING SAUCE**
3 tablespoons hoisin sauce
½ teaspoon chili sauce
6 slices fresh ginger, bruised with the end of a knife
½ cup water
1 clove garlic, pressed

1. To make the filling: In a medium skillet, cook the mushrooms, oil, water, hoisin sauce, and salt over medium heat until the moisture has evaporated, leaving behind the mushrooms in a thick glaze. Allow to cool.

2. In a large saucepan, cook the vermicelli in boiling salted water for about 5 minutes, until tender. Drain.

3. Fill a large mixing bowl half-full with hot tap water. Place 1 sheet of the rice paper into the water. Soak for 30 to 40 seconds.

4. Place a soaked rice paper on a cutting board that has been covered with cheesecloth so that it doesn't slip around. On the third of the rice paper closest to you, arrange the ingredients on top of each other in a thin line in the following order: 2 tablespoons carrot, a lettuce leaf, a few mint leaves, 2 tablespoons bean sprouts, 1½ tablespoons mushrooms, and 2 tablespoons vermicelli.

5. Roll the ingredients as gently and firmly as possible away from you until the half-way point. Then tuck in the loose sides to prevent the ingredients from coming out the ends. Continue rolling until you have a chubby, cigar-shape roll (this takes a little practice to get it right, but it tastes good even if it isn't perfect). Repeat with remaining rice paper and filling.

6. To make the dipping sauce: In a small saucepan, combine all the ingredients. Cook over medium heat until it begins to boil. Remove the pan from the heat and strain out the ginger and garlic and discard. The sauce is ready to use warm or at room temperature.

7. Cut each roll in half and place them on a serving plate with a dish of the dipping sauce.

*eggplant*

# Grilled Eggplant Dip

*Some might say the beauty of California life is that it has little or no tradition save for its Spanish roots. This means that creativity rules, and anything goes. Just look to Hollywood for validation.*

*So in the spirit of the cross-cultural dining experiences, we'll begin with an eggplant dip that takes the Middle Eastern favorite baba ghanoush south of the border.*

**Preparation Time: 30 minutes  ▪  Cooking Time: 15 minutes  ▪  Makes 2 cups**

▪ ▪ ▪

Salt, to taste

1 globe eggplant, sliced into 1-inch-thick slices

4 tablespoons olive oil, plus extra for brushing eggplant

1 pasilla chili pepper

1 red or yellow bell pepper

1 tablespoon minced garlic

1 tablespoon fresh lime juice

1 teaspoon cumin powder

2 tablespoons chopped cilantro (optional)

Freshly ground black pepper, to taste

Tortilla chips, to serve

1. Salt the eggplant slices generously and set aside for about 30 minutes. Rinse the beads of moisture and salt off the eggplant and pat dry with a paper towel. Brush each slice with a little olive oil to keep the eggplant from sticking to the grill. Place the slices on a hot grill. Cook the eggplant until it is soft. Set aside to cool.

2. Grill the chili pepper and bell pepper whole (see page 87), cooking them until the skin has blackened on all sides. Set aside to cool. When the peppers are cool, peel off the blackened skin with your fingers. It should come off easily. Cut the peppers in half, remove the seeds, and finely chop. Set aside.

3. In the bowl of a food processor, combine the eggplant, garlic, lime juice, cumin, 4 tablespoons olive oil, and cilantro (if using). Process until chopped, but not completely smooth. Stir in the peppers. Taste for seasoning, add salt and pepper if needed, and serve with tortilla chips.

# Green Chili Salsa

This green salsa first appeared in my original cookbook, Regina's Vegetarian Table, *and I have been so pleased with the response that I decided to share it again.*

*This is a relatively mild salsa, so if your palate requires something more challenging, just add some habaneros (or scotch bonnet chilies). Be sure to warn your guests, however.*

**Preparation Time: 15 minutes ▪ Cooking Time: 0 ▪ Makes 2½ cups**

▪ ▪ ▪

6 to 7 tomatillos
2 jalapeño chilies
1 small green bell pepper
1½ large sweet onions
1 large clove garlic, minced
1 tablespoon extra-virgin olive oil
½ teaspoon freshly ground black pepper
1 teaspoon freshly ground cumin
½ teaspoon salt

1. Finely chop the tomatillos, jalapeños, bell pepper, and onion in a food processor or by hand. If chopping jalapeños by hand, wear rubber gloves to prevent the juice from burning your skin.

2. Add the garlic, oil, black pepper, cumin, and salt. Mix well. Store in an airtight container in the refrigerator and use as needed. It should last at least a week.

# Artichoke Heart Puffs

*Take the French tradition of* pate au choux *(puff pastry), and add the piquant flavors and textures of artichokes, green olives, lime juice, and cayenne, and you'll discover the most interesting little appetizers this side of Atlanta, but be prepared for requests for more from your guests.*

**Preparation Time: 1 hour** ▪ **Cooking Time: 45 minutes** ▪ **Makes 24 puffs**

▪ ▪ ▪

**ARTICHOKE FILLING**

4 medium artichokes

2 tablespoons lemon juice or vinegar in a bowl of water

⅓ cup pitted green olives

1 tablespoon minced garlic

1 tablespoon finely chopped parsley

1 tablespoon fresh lime juice

3 tablespoons extra-virgin olive oil

Salt and freshly ground black pepper, to taste

Pinch cayenne pepper

**PATE AU CHOUX (PUFFS)**

½ cup (8 tablespoons) unsalted butter

1 cup water

¼ teaspoon salt

1 cup all-purpose flour

4 eggs

¼ cup finely grated Parmesan cheese

1. To make the Artichoke Filling: Trim the artichokes down to the tender hearts and cut in half. Remove the hearts and cut into quarters. As you finish each one, put it into the bowl of water with lemon juice to keep them from turning brown.

2. In a medium saucepan, bring a full pot of water to a boil. Cook the artichoke hearts in the boiling water for about 8 minutes, until tender. Remove the artichokes from the water with a slotted spoon and allow them to cool. When cool, place the artichokes and all the remaining filling ingredients in the bowl of a food processor and process until finely chopped. Set aside.

3. To make the Pate au Choux: Preheat the oven to 375F (190C). Grease two baking sheets.

4. Cut the butter into 8 pieces and combine it with the water and salt in a saucepan. Cook over medium heat until the butter melts and the mixture is boiling. Remove the saucepan from the heat. Add the flour and stir until blended. Return the saucepan to the heat and cook for 4 to 5 minutes, stirring constantly. The mixture should be very thick and no steam should be rising—a sign that excess water has evaporated. Remove the saucepan from the stove and allow it to cool slightly.

5. Break the eggs into the mixture, one at a time, stirring well after each egg. Add the Parmesan cheese and mix well. Spoon onto the baking sheets in heaping tablespoonfuls. Wet your fingers and smooth the dough so it forms nice, smooth shapes.

6. Bake for 25 to 30 minutes, until the puffs are brown. Remove the baking sheets from the oven and pierce each puff with the tip of a small knife. Turn off the oven and return the puffs to the oven for 10 minutes to dry. Remove them from the oven and allow to cool.

7. When cool, split each puff in half with a knife, fill with Artichoke Filling, and place the halves gently back together (sides will not be touching). Serve immediately.

# SALADS
## Just Add Dressing

———— ■ ■ ■ ————

From lentils with feta to tofu molds on greens to rice with vegetables and nuts, it's the combination of oil and vinegar, lemon, yogurt, and seasonings drizzled over the food that turns the dish into a salad. This leaves a tremendous amount of leeway for experimentation in creating your own salads.

For me, a salad always contains some type of fresh produce, be it vegetable or fruit. Combining the crisp texture of freshly chopped bell peppers or celery, juicy tomatoes, fresh tender salad greens, and tangy dressings feels like "life on a plate" for me. In fact, a friend of mine and I were in a rapturous state just the other day when we tasted the first of my Early Girl tomatoes. We sniffed, sliced, and tasted the deliciously fragrant and sweet wedges hot from the sun and just off the vine. Simplicity at its best!

To ensure the freshness of the ingredients, shopping on a more frequent basis is a necessity. Being fickle in my eating habits, this suits my type of temperament, as I don't know what I will want to eat from one meal to the next. Even a couple shopping trips a week will do if your produce is stored properly.

For maximum flavor, I would recommend organic produce, especially that grown on local farms. Care is generally taken to pick the produce when it is ripe rather than while it is still green, and the food is in harmony with your region's growing seasons. This is when produce is at its best.

If you don't have local fresh produce markets, you might consider calling one of the finer restaurants in your area to find out where they get their produce. Perhaps you could be added to a delivery list. If not, natural food stores will generally have a good supply of organic produce, some locally grown, some not.

Subscription-based farming is another option. Go online or inquire at your local natural foods market as to whether or not this service is available in your area. With this option, the local grower delivers a box of just-picked produce to a central location in town, usually a store or somebody's home once or twice a week. This is about as good as growing it yourself.

## Basic Dressing Ingredients

To turn your produce, grains, and nuts into a salad, you'll need to have a variety of salad dressing ingredients on hand. Here's a list of basic ingredients for ethnic-style dressings:

**Italian:** A good wine or balsamic vinegar and extra-virgin olive oil

**French:** Wine vinegar, a good mustard, garlic, and olive oil

**Asian:** Seasoned or plain rice vinegar, peanut oil or other nut oils, shoyu, tamari, miso, and silken tofu for thicker-blended dressings

**Middle Eastern:** Yogurt or buttermilk, lemon juice or a light vinegar, olive oil, fresh herbs such as mint and parsley

Natural sea salt, freshly ground pepper, and spices can be added to all of the above.

■ ■ ■

■ ■ ■

# Avocado-Pineapple Salad
## with Honey-Lime Dressing

*This bright, tropical salad is like a plate of sunshine! The tartness of lime coupled with honey provides a perfect complement for the rich, smooth flavor and texture of the avocado. Use fresh pineapple whenever possible; choose one that has begun to develop pink or red markings on the outside. This indicates full ripeness. In addition, the pineapple should smell sweet, and the leaves should pull out easily.*

**Preparation Time: 15 minutes** ▪ **Cooking Time: 0** ▪ **Makes 4 servings**

▪ ▪ ▪

> ½ small pineapple, cored and sliced
>
> 1 avocado, sliced
>
> 1 tablespoon honey
>
> Juice of 1 lime (2 tablespoons)
>
> 2 tablespoons grapeseed oil or other light-tasting oil
>
> ¼ teaspoon chili powder
>
> ¼ cup chopped fresh cilantro (optional)

1. Arrange the pineapple and avocado decoratively on a platter.

2. In a bowl, whisk together the honey, lime juice, oil, and chili powder. Pour the dressing over the avocado and pineapple. Garnish with cilantro, if desired, and serve.

# Marinated Roasted Beets on Greens

*The composed salad is remarkably satisfying with the earthiness and tang of roasted beets paired with tender greens and the creaminess of the slightly tart yogurt dressing. When you're feeling a bit lethargic, keep in mind that this intensely pigmented vegetable has a wonderfully tonic effect on the blood, assisting in the process of red blood cell production.*

**Preparation Time: 30 minutes ▪ Cooking Time: 40 minutes ▪ Makes 4 servings**

2 small beets, peeled and cut into ½-inch cubes

3 tablespoons extra-virgin olive oil

1 tablespoon white wine vinegar or seasoned rice vinegar

1 tablespoon sliced garlic

Salt and freshly ground black pepper, to taste

**YOGURT DRESSING**

¼ cup plain yogurt

1½ tablespoons seasoned rice vinegar

1 tablespoon extra-virgin olive oil

Salt and freshly ground black pepper, to taste

¼ teaspoon prepared horseradish (optional)

1 head lettuce, such as butter lettuce, washed and torn into bite-size pieces

½ small red onion, thinly sliced

1. Preheat the oven to 325F (165C). Place the beets in a baking dish and drizzle them with the olive oil and vinegar. Add the garlic and season with salt and pepper.

2. Cover the baking dish with aluminum foil. Bake for 40 minutes. Uncover and bake for another 20 minutes.

3. To make the Yogurt Dressing: Whisk together the yogurt, vinegar, oil, salt, pepper, and horseradish in a small bowl. Drizzle the dressing over the lettuce and toss to coat.

4. Spoon the hot beets over the lettuce on individual plates. Garnish with the onion.

# Cucumbers in Savory Sour Cream

*My brother-in-law, Norbert, grew up just a few miles from the Czechoslovakian border in the German countryside. Norbert's father, mother, and aunt tended their garden in the warm months and put the vegetables into the root cellar once the cold weather set in. Part of the summer and fall harvest was reserved for pickling and canning. Rarely did a meal pass that did not have some sort of marinated cucumber on the table.*

*Norbert continued his tradition of marinated cucumbers with sour cream after he immigrated to the United States, slicing garden-fresh cucumbers when he got home from work and readying them for the evening's consumption. Norbert's sour cream cucumbers were the inspiration for this simple and fresh salad.*

**Preparation Time: 20 minutes** ▪ **Cooking Time: 10 minutes** ▪ **Makes 4 servings**

▪ ▪ ▪

½ cup reduced-fat sour cream

¼ cup chopped fresh dill

3 tablespoons seasoned rice vinegar

1 shallot, chopped

½ teaspoon ground toasted caraway seeds (see Note, below)

½ teaspoon salt

¼ teaspoon freshly ground pepper

3 cucumbers, halved, seeded, and thinly sliced

1. Combine all the ingredients except the cucumbers in a medium bowl.

2. Stir in the cucumbers.

**Note:** To toast the caraway seeds, place them in a small skillet over medium heat and warm them, stirring to promote even toasting, for about 10 minutes. You will smell a toasty aroma. Watch carefully that they do not burn. Set aside until cool. Grind in a spice grinder or a clean coffee grinder.

# Tender Greens with Provençal Dressing

One of the characteristics of salads served at the French table is the simplicity of the ingredient list. Often the salad is nothing more than lettuce or tomato and onion. Each home I've visited in France has its version of the family salad dressing. I was taught how to make this dressing many years ago by a French student who came to live with us. It was her mother's version of the classic French oil and vinegar dressing. As simple as this salad appears to be, it's packed with flavor. For a variation, you can add any vegetables, nuts, or other salad ingredients you wish.

**Preparation Time: 10 minutes** ▪ **Cooking Time: 0** ▪ **Makes 2 to 4 servings**

▪ ▪ ▪

2 to 4 cups tender field greens of choice

**PROVENÇAL DRESSING**
3 tablespoons red wine vinegar or 2 tablespoons aged balsamic
    vinegar for a sweeter flavor
1 teaspoon spicy brown mustard
1 clove garlic, minced
⅓ cup extra-virgin olive oil
¼ teaspoon salt
⅛ teaspoon freshly ground black pepper

1. Place the greens in a salad bowl. Set aside.

2. To make the Provençal Dressing: Whisk all the ingredients in a small bowl until combined. Pour the dressing over the greens and toss to coat.

# Artichoke and Rice Salad

*Although this earthy and satisfying salad calls for fresh baby artichokes, you may also use canned or jarred marinated artichoke hearts. Just drain off the oil or water from a 6-ounce jar of artichoke hearts, pat any excess oil off the artichokes, and use as you would fresh artichokes.*

**Preparation Time: 30 minutes** ▪ **Cooking Time: 30 to 45 minutes** ▪ **Makes 6 to 8 servings**

▪ ▪ ▪

1½ pounds baby artichokes (see headnote above)
1 tablespoon minced garlic
1 tablespoon minced fresh oregano
1 tablespoon fresh lemon juice
2 tablespoons seasoned rice vinegar
6 tablespoons extra-virgin olive oil
1 cup cooked wild rice
1 cup cooked brown rice
4 medium tomatoes, cut into wedges
1 cucumber, peeled, seeded, and thinly sliced
Salt and freshly ground black pepper, to taste

1. To prepare the artichokes, remove the tough outside petals. Slice the tops off the artichokes and trim around the bases. Cut the artichokes in half. Slice the artichokes thinly and cook in boiling salted water until tender.

2. In a small bowl, whisk the garlic, oregano, lemon juice, vinegar, and oil until combined. Set aside.

3. Transfer the rice to a serving bowl. Add the tomatoes, cucumber, and artichokes to the rice. Toss with the dressing. Taste for salt and black pepper and add as needed.

# Greek Salad

The pungent flavors of Greek feta cheese and kalamata olives make this simple salad one of the most robust-tasting in the world. If you have a delicate palate and do not care for the bite of traditional Greek feta, replace it with French feta, which not only has a milder flavor, but is also less salty.

**Preparation Time: 15 minutes ■ Cooking Time: 0 ■ Makes 4 servings**

■ ■ ■

> 3 medium tomatoes, cut into wedges
>
> 1 large cucumber, peeled, quartered, and thickly sliced
>
> 2 ounces crumbled feta cheese
>
> ¼ cup kalamata olives, pitted and quartered
>
> ½ small red onion, thinly sliced (optional)
>
> Yogurt Dressing (page 42)

1. Combine the tomatoes, cucumber, cheese, olives, and onion (if using) in a large bowl.

2. Add the dressing and toss to combine. Serve at room temperature.

# Raita (Cucumbers and Yogurt)

*The cool and creamy yogurt makes raita the ideal palate cooler for pungent and spicy dishes.*

**Preparation Time: 60 minutes** ▪ **Cooking Time: 0** ▪ **Makes 4 to 6 servings**

▪ ▪ ▪

1 cup plain yogurt

1 large cucumber, peeled, sliced lengthwise, seeded, and sliced crosswise into chunks

1½ teaspoons fresh lemon juice

½ teaspoon Garam Masala (page 120), or purchased

⅛ teaspoon salt

1. Place the yogurt in a strainer that has been lined with cheesecloth. Set the strainer over a bowl to drain for 1 hour.

2. Put the drained yogurt and remaining ingredients in a blender. Blend until coarsely pureed, allowing some texture to remain.

3. Serve chilled. Store, covered, for up to 2 to 3 days.

# Buffalo Mozzarella and Tomato Salad

*This is my favorite quick lunch in the summertime, when tomatoes are at their best. You can compose this salad in any number of portions you choose. The dish does require that you find a good, fresh buffalo mozzarella, as the standard dry mozzarella at the supermarket is not a good substitute.*

**Preparation Time: 20 minutes ▪ Cooking Time: 0 ▪ Makes 4 servings**

▪ ▪ ▪

2 (8-ounce) balls fresh buffalo mozzarella

4 medium sun-ripened tomatoes, cut into slices

8 to 10 fresh basil leaves, thinly sliced

Extra-virgin olive oil, to taste

Balsamic vinegar, to taste

Salt and freshly ground black pepper, to taste

1. Cut the mozzarella into slices half the thickness of the tomatoes. Arrange the tomatoes and mozzarella, alternating cheese and tomatoes, on a salad plate or large serving platter.

2. Sprinkle the basil over the tomatoes and mozzarella.

3. Drizzle the salad with olive oil and a light dribble of balsamic vinegar. Salt somewhat generously, as the ingredients are quite bland. Sprinkle with freshly ground pepper and serve.

# *Sunomono*

*Sweet and crunchy, this little salad is a very light and refreshing addition to a Japanese meal.*

**Preparation Time: 5 minutes ▪ Cooking Time: 0 ▪ Makes 2 to 3 servings**

▪ ▪ ▪

> 1 large cucumber, peeled and thinly sliced
> ¼ cup seasoned rice vinegar
> 2 tablespoons water

1. Mix the cucumber, vinegar, and water in a bowl. Cover and refrigerate for 30 minutes.

2. Serve chilled.

# Soba Noodle Salad

*The Japanese consume a surprisingly high percentage of noodles in the daily diet. This soba noodle salad is one of the most popular of the noodle dishes. Sesame oil, chili oil, green onions, and roasted cashews give this cold buckwheat noodle salad its pleasant Far Eastern flavor.*

**Preparation Time: 15 minutes • Cooking Time: 0 • Makes 4 servings**

4 ounces soba noodles

2 tablespoons grapeseed oil or peanut oil

1 tablespoon seasoned rice vinegar

1 teaspoon shoyu sauce

8 drops chili oil

8 drops sesame oil

1 green onion (green and white parts), finely chopped

3 tablespoons roasted cashews or peanuts

1. Place the noodles into 4 cups boiling salted water and cook for 5 to 6 minutes. Drain and rinse in cold water.

2. In a small bowl, mix the grapeseed oil, vinegar, shoyu sauce, chili oil, and sesame oil to make a dressing.

3. In a serving bowl, toss together the noodles, dressing, and onion. Top with the cashews. Serve at room temperature.

## Shoyu

Shoyu is the queen of soy sauces. Its four main ingredients are soybeans, wheat, water, and salt. Naturally fermented, shoyu takes two years to make. The result is a much richer soy sauce than is found in the common supermarket varieties. Although shoyu is commonly available in health food stores, you might have to shop around to find it in the supermarket. It costs a little more, but it's well worth the investment.

# Jicama and Strawberry Salad

*Jicama is a much underrated vegetable in the United States. Once you give it a try, I think you'll look forward to integrating this crunchy, cool, and mildly sweet vegetable into your list of staple foods. In this recipe, jicama is paired with strawberries, lime juice, and a little kick of cayenne to create a party of flavors and textures on the tongue. Just be sure to buy your jicama with the smoothest, least-blemished skin available in the market. The fresher they are, the sweeter and more tender they are.*

**Preparation Time: 15 minutes** ▪ **Cooking Time: 0** ▪ **Makes 4 servings**

▪ ▪ ▪

2 to 4 cups fresh mild lettuce greens, such as butter, romaine, and red leaf, torn into bite-size pieces

2 cups peeled, julienned jicama

8 to 12 strawberries, stems removed and sliced

**LIME-HONEY DRESSING**
Juice of 1 lime

1½ to 2 tablespoons honey

2 tablespoons grapeseed oil or other mild oil

Pinch cayenne pepper (optional)

Salt, to taste

1. Arrange the lettuce on a salad plate or large serving platter.

2. Arrange the jicama and sliced strawberries decoratively on top of the lettuce.

3. To make the dressing: Whisk all the dressing ingredients together in a bowl. Drizzle the dressing over the salad and serve.

# Encrusted Tofu on Greens

The popularity of encrusted dishes is surfacing in a variety of ethnic restaurants around the country. In this recipe, we're using tofu as the base of the encrusting ingredients rather than the traditional fish or fowl. Because tofu is on the bland side, a marinade of tamari sauce and ginger is used to add tang and flair to the dish.

**Preparation Time: 10 minutes (plus 24 hours marinating)** ▪ **Cooking Time: 10 minutes** ▪ **Makes 4 servings**

▪ ▪ ▪

> ⅓ cup tamari sauce
>
> 1 tablespoon grated fresh ginger
>
> 8 ounces firm, silken tofu (Japanese style)
>
> ¼ cup slivered, blanched almonds
>
> 4 to 6 saltine crackers, finely crumbled
>
> ¼ pound tender salad greens, washed and dried

1. Place the tamari sauce in a small bowl. Place the ginger into a cheesecloth or tiny strainer and squeeze the ginger juice into the tamari sauce. Stir and set aside.

2. Slice the tofu into ½-inch-thick slices. Place them into a baking dish and pour the tamari sauce over the tofu. Let the tofu marinate overnight in the refrigerator.

3. Preheat the oven to 425F (220C). Place the almonds and crackers together in a food processor. Process until mixture resembles a coarse meal. Place the nut meal onto a small plate.

4. Dredge the tofu slices through the nut meal and pat the meal onto the surface until each slice is coated on both sides. Place them on a nonstick baking sheet.

5. Drizzle each slice with olive oil. Bake for 10 minutes.

6. Remove from the oven and serve hot on the greens.

# Gingered Broccoli and Noodle Salad

*In most of the vegetable dishes in Southeast Asia, you'll find the presence of a little heat. Hot pepper oils and chili flakes were incorporated into the native cuisine through trading, arriving from India by way of Java. The blending of these hot spices with the native ingredients such as soy, sesame, and ginger creates an incredibly complex flavor base to the cuisine.*

**Preparation Time: 30 minutes ▪ Cooking Time: 10 minutes ▪ Makes 6 to 8 servings**

▪ ▪ ▪

3 tablespoons balsamic vinegar

1 tablespoon seasoned rice vinegar

3 tablespoons minced garlic

1 tablespoon grated fresh ginger

Salt, to taste

8 tablespoons shoyu or soy sauce

2 to 3 teaspoons toasted sesame oil

1 tablespoon hot chili oil

2 cups broccoli florets

1 (about 8-ounce) package soba noodles

1 red bell pepper, thinly sliced

1 small cucumber, peeled, quartered lengthwise, seeded, and sliced

1/2 cup coarsely chopped fresh cilantro

1. Whisk the balsamic and rice vinegars, garlic, ginger, salt, and shoyu sauce in a bowl until combined. Whisk in the sesame and chili oils. Set aside.

2. Bring a pot of water to a boil. Add the broccoli, cook for 1 minute, and remove with a slotted spoon. Rinse under cold water. Set aside.

3. Cook the soba noodles in boiling water according to package directions.

4. Toss together the noodles, dressing, pepper, cucumber, and cilantro. Serve warm or at room temperature.

# Strawberry and Almond Salad

*As with any composed salad, there is a lot of latitude for creativity with this salad. The concept here is to combine the fresh tang of strawberries and the crunch of toasted almonds with a bed of spinach drizzled with a lovely fruit vinegar–based dressing—a wonderful accompaniment to a summer lunch or brunch! Just play with the ingredients and amounts and add whatever feels good. For example, a little thinly sliced red onion would also be good here.*

*Extra salad dressing can be saved for future use in a tightly covered container in the refrigerator for up to a month.*

**Preparation Time: 10 to 15 minutes ▪ Cooking Time: 0 ▪ Makes 4 servings**

▪ ▪ ▪

1 pound tender or baby spinach leaves, well washed and dried

1 cup sliced fresh strawberries

4 tablespoons muscat or golden raisins

4 tablespoons slivered almonds, toasted

**BERRY-SCENTED DRESSING**

2½ tablespoons raspberry, blueberry, or balsamic vinegar

⅓ cup walnut, grapeseed, or almond oil

¼ teaspoon salt

¼ teaspoon sugar

¼ teaspoon freshly ground black pepper

1. Arrange the spinach leaves on a salad plate.

2. Top with the strawberries, raisins, and almonds.

3. To make the dressing: Mix all the ingredients together in a small bowl. Drizzle the dressing over the salad and serve.

# Quinoa and Wild Rice Salad with Dried Apricots

*Although quinoa is little known in the northern hemisphere, it has been cultivated in the mountainous regions of Peru and Bolivia for more than 3,000 years. The production dipped for about 500 years with the arrival of Peru's uninvited guests, the Spaniards, but quinoa is back, and lucky for us!*

*Quinoa (pronounced KEEN-wah) has twice the protein of other common grains and is a good source of B vitamins, calcium, and iron. The tiny seeds cook quickly and add a wonderful taste and texture to any grain or vegetable dish. I even like it for breakfast when boiled with toasted buckwheat for a hearty, nutritious start to the day.*

**Preparation Time: 30 minutes  ▪  Cooking Time: 20 minutes  ▪  Makes 4 to 6 servings**

▪ ▪ ▪

5 cups water

¾ cup quinoa

Salt

¾ cup wild rice

Grapeseed or olive oil, for cooking

3 cups thinly sliced mushrooms

⅓ cup chopped chives or green onions

¼ cup chopped fresh parsley

⅓ cup dried currants, golden raisins, or date pieces

¼ cup chopped dried apricots

**SOY DRESSING**

3 tablespoons grapeseed oil or any mild oil

1½ tablespoons shoyu or soy sauce

4 tablespoons seasoned rice vinegar

1. In a small saucepan, bring 2½ cups water to a boil; add the quinoa and ¼ teaspoon salt. Bring it back to a boil, then cover and reduce the heat to low and simmer for 10 minutes. Transfer to a bowl.

2. In another small saucepan, bring the remaining 2½ cups water to a boil. Add the wild rice, bring it back to a boil, then cover and reduce the heat to low and simmer for 15 minutes. Transfer to the bowl with the quinoa and stir to combine.

3. Brush a small skillet with oil. Add the mushrooms and season with salt. Cook the mushrooms over medium-high heat until the mushrooms are tender and the liquid has evaporated.

4. Add the mushrooms, chives, parsley, currants, and apricots to the quinoa mixture.

5. To make the dressing: Whisk the dressing ingredients in a small bowl. Pour the dressing over the grain-fruit mixture. Toss to combine and serve warm.

# Greens and Ricotta Salata
## with Smoky Tomato Dressing

*The secret to this simple salad, which takes some of its inspiration from Greek fare, is the Smoky Tomato Dressing. I was exposed to this dressing by John Ash, winner of the Julia Child Award for his beautiful cookbook* From the Earth to the Table *(Dutton, 1995), when he joined me as a guest on my television program. One of the things I love about John is his ability to make do without a lot of fuss. The feature on smoking tomatoes using simple items to create your own smoker without a big investment (page 26) is an example of his resourcefulness in the kitchen.*

**Preparation Time: 30 minutes** ▪ **Cooking Time: 20 minutes** ▪ **Makes 4 servings**

▪ ▪ ▪

**SMOKY TOMATO DRESSING**

2 medium tomatoes

3 tablespoons extra-virgin olive oil

3 tablespoons seasoned rice vinegar

1/8 teaspoon salt

Freshly ground black pepper, to taste

Sprinkling of cayenne pepper (optional)

1 pound lettuce, such as romaine, radicchio, endive, or arugula, washed and torn into bite-size pieces

8 thin slices ricotta salata cheese (see Note below)

3 cups thinly sliced red onions

1/2 cup ripe olives, your favorite kind, cut into wedges or sliced

1. To make the Smoky Tomato Dressing: Smoke the tomatoes according to the directions on page 26. Remove the skins, cut out the cores, and place the tomatoes in a food processor. Puree until smooth.

2. Pour the tomato puree through a fine mesh strainer to remove the seeds and large pieces of pulp or skin. You should end up with approximately ⅓ cup tomato puree.

3. In a small bowl, combine the tomato puree and the remaining dressing ingredients. Use immediately or cover and refrigerate up to 3 days.

4. On individual salad plates or a large serving platter, arrange the lettuce and top with the ricotta, sliced onions, and olives.

5. Drizzle the dressing over the salad and serve.

**Note:** Ricotta salata is an aged ricotta that has a mild flavor and slightly dry texture. If you're having a difficult time finding ricotta salata, it can be replaced with a Mexican cheese called queso anejo or panela. A mild feta cheese would also work.

# Garlic Lovers' Pasta Salad

*This pasta salad is a runaway favorite at the Sacramento Natural Foods Co-Op in Sacramento, California. But beware! When we say garlic lovers' pasta, we mean enough garlic to boost the immune system of a small village. Yum!*

**Preparation Time: 30 minutes ▪ Cooking Time: 15 minutes ▪ Makes 6 servings**

▪ ▪ ▪

1 pound pasta, such as corkscrew, butterfly, or elbow

**CREAMY DRESSING**
¾ cup mayonnaise
1½ tablespoons fresh lemon juice
1 to 1½ tablespoons minced garlic
½ teaspoon salt

½ pound fresh or frozen peas, rinsed and drained
⅔ cup grated dry cheese, such as dry Jack, Pecorino, or aged Gouda

1. Cook the pasta according to the package directions. Rinse with cold water and set aside.

2. To make the dressing: In a small bowl, whisk together the mayonnaise, lemon juice, garlic, and salt.

3. Toss the dressing with the pasta. Add the peas and toss to combine. Add the cheese, saving some to garnish the top, and toss to combine.

# Green Bean and Mushroom Salad

*Simple and crunchy, this green bean salad features just enough garlic and balsamic to give it flair. A slight sweetness from the dressing and a sprinkling of toasted almonds finish off this delightful little salad.*

**Preparation Time: 30 minutes** ▪ **Cooking Time: 10 minutes** ▪ **Makes 4 servings**

▪ ▪ ▪

½ pound green beans, ends removed, cut into 1- to 2-inch pieces
Salt and freshly ground black pepper, to taste

**DRESSING**
1½ tablespoons seasoned rice vinegar
2 tablespoons grapeseed or olive oil
Salt and freshly ground black pepper, to taste

½ pound mushrooms, sliced
2 cloves garlic, pressed
¼ cup water or vegetable broth
2 teaspoons balsamic vinegar
2 to 3 tablespoons slivered almonds, toasted

1. Steam the green beans in a steamer for 3 to 4 minutes, until crisp-tender. Remove the beans from the steamer and place them in a bowl of ice cold water for 1 minute. Drain off the water and place them in a bowl. Season with salt and pepper.

2. To make the dressing: Whisk together the vinegar, oil, salt, and pepper in a small bowl.

3. Pour the dressing over the green beans and mix well. Let stand for 30 minutes, stirring occasionally.

4. Meanwhile, place the mushrooms, garlic, water, and vinegar in a small skillet and cook over medium heat until the mushrooms are tender and the liquid has evaporated. Remove from the heat and allow them to cool.

5. Combine the mushrooms and the beans and top with the almonds.

# Honey-Mustard Coleslaw

*This is not the bland, creamy-style coleslaw you'll find at the grocery store deli counter. Rather, it is a colorful, sweet, and crunchy treat for the mouth.*

*Apples, pine nuts, and red onion complement the healthful attributes of cabbage, with honey and mustard adding the finishing touch to this coleslaw.*

**Preparation Time: 30 minutes ▪ Cooking Time: 0 ▪ Makes 6 to 8 servings**

▪ ▪ ▪

½ small green cabbage, shredded

½ small red cabbage, shredded

1 small red onion, diced

1 cup pine nuts

1 large apple, peeled, halved, cored, and diced

**HONEY-MUSTARD DRESSING**

3 tablespoons mustard

3 tablespoons honey

¼ cup white wine vinegar or plain rice vinegar

1 teaspoon celery seed

2 tablespoons olive oil

Salt and freshly ground black pepper, to taste

1. Place the green and red cabbages, onion, pine nuts, and apple in a large mixing bowl.

2. To make the Honey-Mustard Dressing: In a small bowl, mix the mustard and honey. Add the remaining ingredients and mix well.

3. Pour the dressing over the slaw ingredients and toss well. Serve immediately for a crunchy slaw. The slaw can be stored for a day or so in an airtight container in the refrigerator, although it will lose some of its crunch.

# Greens and Hickory Tofu Molds

*This dish is so flavorful that you may find yourself craving greens as if they were your favorite chocolates! In short, there is nothing boring about these collard greens. We have hickory-smoked tofu to thank, which brings the down-home flavor of the smoked meats traditionally used in Southern cooking. The tofu also adds additional texture and protein to the dish.*

**Preparation Time: 30 minutes** ▪ **Cooking Time: 10 minutes** ▪ **Makes 4 servings**

▪ ▪ ▪

1 small onion, diced

2 cloves garlic, minced

2 bunches collard greens or other favorite greens, stemmed, washed, and coarsely chopped

2 tablespoons butter

Pinch nutmeg, preferably freshly grated

Salt and freshly ground black pepper, to taste

3 ounces hickory baked tofu, crumbled

¼ cup half-and-half or fat-free evaporated milk

1. In a medium saucepan over medium heat, cook the onion and garlic in ½ cup water for 3 to 5 minutes, until tender. Add the greens and cook, adding small amounts of water if necessary, until the greens are completely wilted. Add the butter, nutmeg, salt, and pepper.

2. Transfer the greens mixture to a food processor and add the tofu and half-and-half. Process until the mixture has a finely ground consistency. Return the mixture to the saucepan and heat until hot, stirring occasionally.

3. To form the molds, pat spoonfuls of the mixture into four small molds or baking cups and turn them over onto individual plates. Serve hot.

# SOUP'S ON!

---

Soups are one of a cook's most reliable friends. Whether they are fancy, simple, quiet, or vibrant, just like the other friends in our lives, you can rely on the comfort soups provide. You can start with soup, like a simple and healthful miso soup, consumed for breakfast, lunch, or dinner in Japan. You can end with it, as with our dessert of Fruit Soup with Sabayon. Or it can be featured at the center of a meal, as demonstrated with our rich and hearty Wild Mushroom Soup with Créme Fraîche.

There are few rules with soups, and you can stretch your imagination to the cosmos for creative new twists on new or old favorites. I will, however, pass on a few tips to make your creative endeavors simpler.

First is the matter of broth. Purists will say that you must have a homemade broth to make good soup. For the most part, I disagree. We're not hanging out the laundry while our stocks are simmering anymore. We have a much faster pace to keep up with in this "age of convenience." However, if you do have the time to make broth from scratch, make extra and freeze it.

One bone I have picked with a number of chefs is their insistence on using poultry or meat stocks in all of their soups. Their argument is that this is the only way to achieve a rich flavor. I have found the same result can be had by simply adding a little olive oil to your broth.

A broth can be as simple as onions, carrots, celery, herbs, and salt simmered together. Fortunately, there is an array of options if you don't have time to make your own stock, such as the following:

**Broths in Aseptic Packaging** These come in a variety of flavors, from organic vegetable broth to roasted vegetable to mushroom. These are handy because you can reseal the container and keep it in the refrigerator for the next use, or up to three days.

**Canned Broths** Canned broths have been available for decades and many are quite good, but they can be salty.

**Bouillon Cubes** These can add an especially zesty taste to a soup, depending on the concentrations you choose to use. Many varieties are available at your health food store. There you will find both domestic and international bouillon cubes with a huge array of flavors. Some are salted and some are not.

**Soup Concentrates in Jars** One of my favorite products is an organic mushroom concentrate in a paste form. The flavors are incredibly rich, and it makes a great broth.

**Powdered Mushrooms** can also be used for mushroom broth by grinding them to a fine powder in a coffee grinder and simmering them along with onions, garlic, and your favorite herbs. This makes a broth saturated in flavor.

## THICKENING AGENTS

When making thick, pureed soups, the thickening agents can range from a béchamel sauce to arrowroot to pureed potatoes. The béchamel sauce does not need to add loads of fat to the recipe, as it can be made with low-fat dairy or vegan ingredients.

## Caribbean Vegetable Stew

*The use of cinnamon and cloves is common in both sweet and savory dishes in the Caribbean Islands. These spices, along with ginger, garlic, and sweet potatoes, give this stew a delightfully tropical flair. When selecting the plantain, choose one that has developed black mottling on the peel if possible. Unlike its cousin, the banana, plantains are tougher, more fibrous, and used for cooking only. The lightly pink or yellow fruit can be boiled, baked, sautéed, or mashed.*

**Preparation Time: 45 minutes ▪ Cooking Time: 45 minutes ▪ Makes 4 to 6 servings**

1 plantain, skin mottled black

1 medium onion, chopped

1 red bell pepper, chopped

1 fresh mild chili pepper, seeded, membrane removed, and chopped

1 small butternut squash, cubed

1 sweet potato, cubed

4 cups vegetable broth

2 cups coarsely pureed, peeled fresh or canned tomatoes

1 tablespoon grated fresh ginger

2 tablespoons chopped garlic

¼ teaspoon ground cinnamon

¼ teaspoon ground cloves

2 small summer squash, cubed

2 tablespoons soy sauce

2 tablespoons fresh lime juice

1½ teaspoons salt, or to taste

Chopped fresh cilantro, for garnish (optional)

1. Peel the plantain, slice lengthwise, and cut the slices into ¼-inch-thick pieces. Simmer the plantain in a pot of boiling water for about 15 minutes. Drain.

2. Meanwhile, in a pan, heat ¼ cup water over medium heat. Add the onion and cook, stirring, for about 5 minutes, until the onion is softened.

3. Add the bell pepper, chili pepper, butternut squash, sweet potato, vegetable broth, tomatoes, ginger, garlic, cinnamon, and cloves to the pan. Cover, reduce the heat to low, and simmer for about 15 minutes, until the vegetables are tender.

4. Add the summer squash and plantain, and cook, stirring, for 5 to 6 minutes, until the summer squash is tender.

5. Add the soy sauce, lime juice, and salt. Garnish with cilantro (if using) and serve hot.

# Chinese Raviolis in Vegetable Broth

*There are few dishes more sensuous than the feeling of these thin-skinned "raviolis" sliding through the lips and across the tongue. Steaming with the flavors of garlic, sesame oil, and Chinese five-spice, this soup is perfect served on a frosty winter evening along with Egg Fu Yong (page 99) or Mu Shu Vegetables (page 96) for a filling meal.*

**Preparation Time: 60 minutes ▪ Cooking Time: 15 minutes ▪ Makes 6 servings**

▪ ▪ ▪

**FILLING**

1 cup peeled eggplant cubes

1/2 cup fresh bamboo shoots

1/2 cup sliced shiitake mushrooms

1/2 (8-ounce) package baked tofu, preferably Asian flavored

1 teaspoon Chinese five-spice powder

2 tablespoons soy sauce

2 teaspoons sesame oil

3 cloves garlic, chopped

3 green onions (greens and whites), chopped

1 (12-ounce) package wonton wrappers

**VEGETABLE BROTH**

3 cups vegetable broth

1 cup water

1/4 cup dry white wine

3 tablespoons minced garlic

2 tablespoons soy sauce

1 teaspoon minced fresh ginger

2 green onions (greens and white parts), minced

1. To make the filling: Place the eggplant, bamboo shoots, mushrooms, tofu, five-spice powder, soy sauce, oil, garlic, and onions into a food processor and chop until coarsely chopped, but leave some texture; do not puree.

2. On a work surface, place about a teaspoonful of the chopped filling in the center of a wonton wrapper. Moisten the edges with a little water. Fold wrapper diagonally into a triangle shape. Pinch lightly to seal the edges. Next, bring two of the corners together, moisten with water, and pinch to seal the edges. Repeat with remaining filling; you will have a few wrappers left over. Place the wontons on a tray in a single layer until you are ready to place them in the broth.

3. To make the Vegetable Broth: In a pot, mix the broth, water, white wine, garlic, soy sauce, and ginger and bring to a simmer. Add the wontons and simmer for about 10 to 12 minutes, until the wontons are cooked. Do not boil the wontons or they will break apart. Add the green onions just before serving.

# *borscht*

## Madame Bovie's Borscht

*Little more needs to be said than that this borscht recipe was met each year with great anticipation at the Russian Orthodox Easter celebration in Madame Bovie's church. Born in Russia, married to a Frenchman, and tutored at the Cordon Bleu, Madame used the resourcefulness of a girl who fled Russia on foot alongside her mother during the Bolshevik Revolution and the skill of a French chef to concoct her favorite dishes. I only wish we could have spent more time together in the kitchen. I miss her innovative spirit and Aunty Mame flair.*

**Preparation Time: 30 minutes** ■ **Cooking Time: 4 to 6 hours** ■ **Makes 8 to 12 servings**

■ ■ ■

2 onions, diced

½ cup water

2 (14.5-ounce) cans julienned beets, drained, or 4 cups julienned, peeled fresh beets

1 fresh turnip, peeled and diced

3 carrots, peeled and sliced

1 large potato, diced

1 head cabbage, sliced thinly

2 cups chopped fresh or canned tomatoes

32-ounce bottle tomato-vegetable juice cocktail

¼ cup balsamic vinegar

3 tablespoons sugar

3 cups water

¼ cup extra-virgin olive oil

Salt and freshly ground black pepper, to taste

6-ounce can tomato paste

Sour cream, for garnish

1. Cook the onions and water in a large soup pot over medium heat until the onions are softened. Add the beets, turnip, carrots, potato, cabbage, tomatoes, tomato-vegetable juice cocktail, vinegar, sugar, water, oil, salt, and pepper.

2. Simmer for 4 to 6 hours, or overnight in a slow cooker. This soup improves in flavor the longer it cooks. About an hour before it is finished cooking, stir in the tomato paste.

3. Serve hot, garnished with a spoonful of sour cream.

## Russian Tea

When entering a Russian dining room or kitchen, one of the most noticeable items would be the samovar, an often ornate metal vessel that keeps the day's supply of tea hot. Families hand down their samovars from one generation to the next. A samovar can be small enough to service a family or waist-high, containing enough rich, dark tea to serve an entire Russian Orthodox congregation.

The tea habit began nearly 400 years ago when traders transported the coveted leaves over land from China by camel. The arduous journey took 18 months. The Russians quickly embraced it as a panacea that could cure nearly every ailment. As the populace became familiar with tea, they developed a preference for a more earthy tea with a suggestion of smoke. To achieve the flavor, they blended Chinese oolong or black tea with souchong, or smoked tea. The mixture of the two became what's known as Russian caravan tea.

Russians drink this tea without milk, but will take a lump of sugar or spoonful of jam into their mouths before sipping the tea. As in the English tradition, tea is often served in the afternoon with cake and pastries in the cooler months.

# Wild Mushroom Soup with Crème Fraîche

*I'm always in search of the perfect cream of mushroom soup, but my search has ended here. I invite you to try this soup and let me know if you have had better, suggesting what I might do to improve it. Although it does call for a dollop of crème fraîche, it can be omitted without losing any flavor.*

**Preparation Time: 30 minutes ▪ Cooking Time: 1 hour ▪ Makes 4 to 6 servings**

▪ ▪ ▪

1 leek, white part only, sliced into chunks

1 cup chopped onion

3 tablespoons butter

8 ounces button mushrooms, sliced

½ cup white wine

Salt and freshly ground black pepper, to taste

6 cups water

⅔ cup dried field mushrooms, ground (opposite)

1 bouquet garni (see page 107)

1 cup sliced carrots

4 ounces wild mushrooms, sliced

Dollop of crème fraîche or Devonshire cream (optional)

1. Cook the leek, onion, and 2 tablespoons of the butter in a skillet over medium-high heat until they are softened. Add the button mushrooms and wine. Cook until the mushrooms are tender and only a small amount of liquid is remaining. Season with salt and pepper. Set aside.

2. In a soup pot, combine the water, ground mushrooms, and bouquet garni. Bring to a slow boil and cook until the liquid reduces by a third. Strain the mixture, reserving the broth and discarding the solids.

3. Combine the broth with the mushroom-onion mixture. Add the carrots and simmer over low heat, covered, for 20 minutes.

4. In a skillet, sauté the wild mushrooms in the remaining 1 tablespoon butter until the mushrooms are tender. Set aside.

5. Place the soup mixture in a blender or food processor and blend until it is smooth. Add the wild mushrooms and season with salt and pepper.

6. Serve hot with a dollop of crème fraîche (if using).

## Extra-Strength Mushroom Broth

I was in the kitchen of Diane Forley of Verbena in New York City shooting a cooking program when I learned how to make the most intensely flavored mushroom broth I had ever tasted. This method of making mushroom broth has now become a standard in both soups and sauces in my kitchen.

First, you need to find a good supplier of dried mushrooms. Ideally, you can buy them in bulk. This is often easier to find in ethnic shops such as Italian of French food shops. This is not necessarily a quality issue, but rather a cost issue, as dried mushrooms can be expensive. The good news is that you'll need no more than 1 or 2 ounces of dried mushrooms to make enough broth for a substantial soup recipe.

Simply grind up the dried mushrooms in an electric coffee grinder until they reach a gritty, powdery texture. Pour the ground mushrooms into a pot of water along with a bouquet garni (see page 107) and perhaps some shallots, and simmer until the liquid is reduced by a third, 20 to 30 minutes. Strain out the mushroom pulp, bouquet garni, and shallots. The remaining rich, brown liquid is ready to use as a base for soups, sauces, or stews.

For a special twist, add a little red or white wine during the cooking process or even a dash of Pernod.

# Citrus-Tomato Rice Soup

*This clean, light, citrus-flavored soup is the perfect starter for a full-course Greek meal when served in small portions. The jasmine rice gives enough body, however, to place this at the center of a lighter meal, served for lunch alongside the Greek Salad (page 47).*

**Preparation Time: 30 minutes** ▪ **Cooking Time: 25 minutes** ▪ **Makes 4 to 6 servings**

▪ ▪ ▪

4 cups vegetable broth

1 cup water

4 cloves garlic, minced

3 cups cooked jasmine or other long-grain rice

¼ to ⅓ cup fresh lemon juice, or to taste

Salt and white pepper, to taste

1 tomato, peeled, seeded, and cut into small cubes

1 tablespoon chopped fresh dill

1. In a soup pot, bring the broth and water to a boil.

2. Add the garlic, rice, lemon juice, salt, and white pepper. Reduce the heat to low. Simmer for 5 minutes.

3. Just before serving, stir in the tomato and dill.

# Curried Cauliflower Soup

*As an alternative to the classic starter of dahl in an Indian meal, we have created this wonderful, zesty cauliflower soup. Ginger, garlic, and cayenne make this a soup to remember and one that can easily be served as an entrée for a luncheon. Serve with pappadams (see below), and your taste buds will be in heaven.*

**Preparation Time: 20 minutes ▪ Cooking Time: 30 minutes ▪ Makes 6 servings**

▪ ▪ ▪

1 medium onion, diced

6 to 8 slices fresh ginger

3 cloves garlic, sliced

1 large tomato, chopped

Water or vegetable broth

Pinch cayenne pepper,
   to taste

1 teaspoon sea salt

Freshly ground black pepper,
   to taste

1 teaspoon curry powder

4 cups vegetable broth

1 cup water

1 small head cauliflower,
   chopped

2 tablespoons extra-virgin olive
   oil or peanut oil (optional)

1. Add the onion, ginger, garlic, and tomato to a large saucepan. Add

## Pappadams

Pappadams are the wafer-thin crispy bread that is served when you sit down to an Indian meal. They are made from ground lentils and generally have a generous amount of pepper and other spices. To enjoy this crunchy treat with your meal, I would suggest you go to a Middle Eastern or Indian specialty shop and purchase pre-made pappadams. All you need to do is place them in the oven at 400F (205C) for a few minutes, until you see little bubbles appear. They can also be fried, but the texture and flavor of the baked version leaves little reason to resort to frying.

just enough water to cover the vegetables. Cook over medium heat until most of the liquid has evaporated.

2. Add the cayenne pepper, salt, black pepper, and curry powder, and cook for 1 minute.

3. Add the 4 cups broth, 1 cup water, and cauliflower. Cook over medium heat for 10 to 15 minutes, until the cauliflower is soft.

4. Place the mixture in a blender. Add the oil (if using) and puree until smooth. Serve hot.

# *Riboletta*

## (TUSCAN BEAN SOUP)

*The following soup is native to Florence, Italy, where steaming bowls are served at the beginning of the meal. Earthy and hearty, this is a big soup for big appetites. My special flare is to give the beans, bread, and vegetables a little uptown dousing of brandy at the end, to impart a rich and elegant flavor to this traditional workingman's fare.*

**Preparation Time: 30 minutes ▪ Cooking Time: 2 hours ▪ Makes 6 to 8 servings**

▪ ▪ ▪

2 cups French bread cubes

10 cups water

1 medium onion, diced

¾ cup finely chopped celery

4 cubes vegetable bouillon

1 cup dried white beans, such as navy or cannellini beans, soaked overnight and drained

4 cups chopped cabbage

½ teaspoon ground cumin

Salt and freshly ground black pepper, to taste

2 tablespoons brandy

Freshly grated Parmesan cheese

1. Place the bread cubes on a baking sheet and bake at 375F (190C) for 10 minutes. Set aside.

2. In a soup pot, bring the water to a boil. Add the onion, celery, bouillon cubes, and beans. Cook for 1 to 1½ hours, uncovered, until the beans are soft.

3. Add the cabbage and cumin and simmer for 10 to 15 minutes, until the cabbage is soft. Season with salt and pepper. Add the brandy and remove the pot from the stove.

4. Place a few bread cubes in the bottom of each bowl. Ladle the soup over the bread and top with cheese. Serve hot.

## Miso Soup

*The beauty of miso soup is that it can be made in little more than the time required to make a cup of tea. Miso paste lasts for weeks, even months in the refrigerator, so invest in a quality brand. I prefer yellow miso, as it has a medium-bodied flavor, but there are several styles available, red being the strongest in flavor and most commonly used in miso soup.*

**Preparation Time: 10 minutes ▪ Cooking Time: 2 minutes ▪ Makes 1 serving**

▪ ▪ ▪

1 cup vegetable or mushroom broth (see page 75)

1 tablespoon chopped green onion (green part only)

2 tablespoons soft tofu cubes

2 tablespoons miso paste

Splash of shoyu, if a more salty flavor is desired

### Miso

This soybean paste, part of the Japanese diet for thirteen centuries, is packed with nutrition. Miso is made by cooking soybeans in salted water, then inoculating the beans with a bacterial culture. This culture breaks down the soybeans and any grain that may accompany it into a flavorful paste that is rich in protein, minerals, and B vitamins; is low in fat; and contains no cholesterol. The bacterial cultures in miso aid in digestion and may enhance the immune system against some bacterial diseases. You can add it to soups, stews, and sauces. Miso is generally found in the refrigerated section of health food stores.

1. In a medium saucepan, bring the broth, onion, and tofu to a boil and cook for 2 minutes.

2. Turn off the heat and add the miso. Allow the soup to sit for about 2 minutes. It is important that you do not cook the miso, as its important enzymes can be destroyed by excessive heat. Adjust the saltiness by adding shoyu to taste. Serve hot.

**Variation** If you do not have tofu on hand or do not care for it, substitute a beaten egg slowly drizzled into the boiling soup, stirring as you drizzle to create a string effect.

# Avocado Sopa de Lima

*In this light and fresh starter to the meal, fresh avocado adds a creamy texture as the finishing ingredient while the freshly squeezed lime juice lends a unique sparkle to this spicy rice soup.*

**Preparation Time: 15 minutes ▪ Cooking Time: 30 minutes ▪ Makes 4 to 6 servings**

▪ ▪ ▪

2 cups water
Salt, to taste
1 cup white rice
3 cups vegetable broth
1 cup water
½ teaspoon ground cumin
1 teaspoon chili powder
1 tablespoon chopped garlic
1 avocado, cut into cubes
Juice of 1 lime

1. Bring 2 cups water and salt to a boil in a saucepan. Add the rice, bring back to a boil. Cover, reduce the heat to low, and simmer for 20 minutes.

2. In a medium saucepan, simmer the broth, remaining 1 cup water, cumin, chili powder, garlic, and rice over medium-high heat just until warmed through.

3. Just before serving, stir in the avocado. Add the lime juice a little at a time, tasting, to prevent the soup from becoming too tart. Stir gently and serve hot.

# Carrot-Cumin Soup

*Root vegetables and savory spices are at the base of many wonderful Mediterranean dishes. In that tradition, we combine sweet, fresh carrots and freshly ground cumin to make a simple yet delightful soup.*

**Preparation Time: 10 minutes ▪ Cooking Time: 25 minutes ▪ Makes 4 to 6 servings**

▪ ▪ ▪

> 1 cup finely chopped onion
>
> 1/2 cup water
>
> 1½ pounds carrots, peeled and cut into 1-inch chunks
>
> 3 cups vegetable broth
>
> 1 cup water
>
> 2 teaspoons freshly ground cumin
>
> Salt and freshly ground black pepper, to taste

1. In a medium skillet, cook the onion and water over medium-high heat for 5 to 8 minutes, until the onion is softened.

2. Add the carrots, broth, water, and cumin. Reduce the heat to low and simmer until the carrots are tender.

3. Place the mixture in a blender or food processor and puree until smooth. If the soup is too thick, add a little more broth or water during the blending. Season with salt and pepper. Serve hot.

# Spicy Pineapple and Coconut Milk Soup

*The most popular dish at the most popular restaurant in the small town I call home is its coconut milk soup. Whether served with fish, fowl, tofu, or vegetables, this soup is often the most popular item on the menu in Southeast Asian restaurants. In our version, fresh pineapple gives a special sparkle to this favorite. You're going to need access to an Asian specialty shop, or to shop online for exotic ingredients, such as green curry paste. Most of the ingredients, however, can be found in a good supermarket.*

**Preparation Time: 20 minutes ▪ Cooking Time: 25 minutes ▪ Makes 6 servings**

▪ ▪ ▪

1 tablespoon chopped shallot

1 tablespoon minced garlic

1 teaspoon toasted sesame oil

2 tablespoons finely chopped red bell pepper

3 cups vegetable broth

2 cups canned coconut milk (unsweetened)

1 cup sliced fresh mushrooms

1 cup chopped fresh pineapple

1 teaspoon green curry paste

1 teaspoon grated fresh ginger

2 lemongrass stalks

2 teaspoons fresh lime juice

Salt and freshly ground black pepper, to taste

1. In a large skillet, cook the shallot, garlic, and sesame oil over medium-high heat for about 5 minutes, until the shallot is soft. Add the bell pepper, vegetable broth, coconut milk, mushrooms, pineapple, curry paste, and ginger.

2. Place the lemongrass stalks on a cutting board. Trim off any brown areas and the top 3 inches of the stalk. With the dull edge of your knife or a meat tenderizer, crush the lemongrass stalks to release the flavor. Add the lemongrass to the soup.

3. Cook the soup for about 15 minutes, until the mushrooms and bell pepper are tender. Remove the lemongrass. Add the lime juice. Season with salt and pepper. Serve hot.

# Garden Pesto Soup with Pine Nuts

*If you've ever had a love affair with minestrone soup, then you will love this fresher and lighter version. Loads of fresh basil and parsley are flash-sautéed and then spooned into the center of this garden-fresh soup to be mixed in after serving. Add a sprinkling of Parmigiano-Reggiano cheese and toasted pine nuts and you'll have a new soup favorite!*

**Preparation Time: 30 minutes** ▪ **Cooking Time: 25 minutes** ▪ **Makes 6 servings**

▪ ▪ ▪

1⅓ cups diced carrots

1 large onion, diced

1 green bell pepper, diced

2 stalks celery, chopped

1 cup water

1 teaspoon seasoning salt

½ teaspoon ground cumin

1 teaspoon chili powder

2 medium tomatoes, chopped

2 medium yellow crookneck squash or zucchini, diced

6 cups vegetable broth

⅓ cup olive oil

1 cup chopped fresh parsley

1 cup chopped fresh basil

½ cup finely shredded Parmesan cheese, preferably Parmigiano-Reggiano

½ cup pine nuts, toasted

1. Cook the carrots, onion, bell pepper, and celery in the water for 7 to 8 minutes, until the vegetables have begun to soften.

2. Stir in the seasoning salt, cumin, and chili powder. Add the tomatoes and squash, along with more water so the vegetables do not stick to the pan, and cook another 5 minutes, until the squash has begun to soften.

3. Add the vegetable broth and bring to a boil. Reduce heat to medium and simmer for 5 to 6 minutes.

4. Meanwhile, heat the olive oil over medium heat. Add the parsley and basil and quickly sauté. Remove from the heat.

5. To serve, ladle the soup into individual soup bowls, place a tablespoonful of the herbs in the center. Sprinkle the Parmesan and pine nuts on top.

# Roasted Pepper Soup

*Bell peppers are the hallmark of Cajun and Creole cuisine. In this recipe, you have the option of red, orange, or yellow bell peppers, each imparting their own color and flavor to this zesty soup. Pair the peppers with chilies and bouquet garni, and you will begin to see the Creole influence.*

**Preparation Time: 45 minutes ▪ Cooking Time: 45 minutes ▪ Makes 4 servings**

▪ ▪ ▪

6 red, orange, or yellow bell peppers, halved, cored, and seeded

2 cups diced onions

2 cloves garlic, sliced

Bouquet garni (page 107)

⅛ to ¼ teaspoon chili flakes

4 cups vegetable broth

Salt, to taste

1. Place the pepper halves, skin side down, directly onto the flame of the burner, until charred. This can also be done in the broiler. Place the charred peppers in a bowl, cover, and set aside for 30 minutes. The skins will peel off easily with your fingers. Reserve the amber-colored liquid in the bottom of the bowl, as it is rich in flavor.

2. In a medium skillet, cook the onions, garlic, bouquet garni, chili flakes, and broth over medium heat for 10 to 12 minutes. Discard the bouquet garni.

3. Pour the broth and the peppers into a blender and puree. Season with salt. Serve hot.

**Variation** For a richer flavor, the soup can be drizzled with olive oil and stirred well just before serving.

Serve chilled instead of hot.

**Roasted Pepper Soup with Rice** Serve the soup over 1½ cups cooked rice, such as a packaged spiced rice mix or rice cooked in herbs and broth.

## Roasting Peppers

There are endless possibilities for roasting your own bell peppers and green chilies. You don't have to roast them at all, because they are available in the supermarket packaged in jars. Assuming you would like to do it yourself, here are some simple suggestions.

First you want to cut the peppers into halves or quarters, removing the ribs and seeds. From here you can put them on an outdoor grill, indoor grill, under the broiler, or on the burners of a gas range. You need to char the outside skin. Once this has been done, place the peppers in a bowl and cover. Let stand for 20 to 30 minutes, allowing the peppers to continue steaming. In this process, the charred skin becomes very loose. Simply remove the skin with your fingers and the peppers are ready to use.

During the height of the pepper season when they are selling for ten for a dollar, roast extra peppers and freeze for later use.

# Roasted Corn Soup

*Crunchy fried okra gives this corn chowder a dramatic final presentation. As you may know from reading my cookbooks, I generally do not fry foods. It seems, however, this was one place it is worth making an exception. You'll understand why when you try it.*

**Preparation Time: 1 hour ▪ Cooking Time: 30 minutes ▪ Makes 6 to 8 servings**

7 ears fresh corn

½ cup plus 2 tablespoons water

3 tablespoons olive oil

3 tablespoons all-purpose flour

1 medium yellow onion, minced

6 cups vegetable broth

1 teaspoon seasoning salt

1 teaspoon ground cumin

2 tablespoons minced fresh oregano

1 red bell pepper, roasted, cored, seeded, and diced (page 87)

4-ounce can diced mild green chilies

½ pound okra

Cornmeal, for coating

Mild oil, for frying

Salt, to taste

1. Place the corn, with husks on, on a gas or charcoal grill and cook on all sides, turning about every 5 minutes, until the husks begin to brown evenly. (If a grill is not available, you can use boiled or steamed corn.) When cool enough to touch, remove the husks, stand the each ear of corn on one end, and cut off the kernels with a serrated knife. Place the ½ cup water and the kernels of one cob in a food processor. Puree until smooth and set aside.

2. In a small skillet, combine the olive oil and flour into a smooth paste to make a roux. Cook over medium-low heat for about 10 minutes, stirring constantly. Set aside.

3. Add the onion and the 2 tablespoons water to a soup pot and cook over medium-high heat until the onion is soft. Add the roux, pureed corn, and broth and bring to a boil. Reduce the heat to low, add the seasoning salt, cumin, oregano, remaining corn kernels, bell pepper, and chilies and warm through.

4. Meanwhile, slice the okra into ½-inch pieces, rinse well, pat dry with a paper towel, and coat with the cornmeal. Heat about 2 inches of oil in a small skillet until very hot. Add the coated okra and fry until crunchy. Sprinkle with salt. Drain the okra quickly on a paper towel.

5. Serve the soup hot, garnished with crunchy fried okra.

# Smoked Tomato and Spinach Soup

*Smoke is the signature flavor of Southwestern cuisine. Sprinkle on a little chili pepper, cumin, and garlic, and you have a base that can be used for a panoply of dishes. The following recipe features smoked tomatoes, spinach, and blue corn tortilla chips for a zesty little meal in a bowl.*

**Preparation Time: 30 minutes ▪ Cooking Time: 10 minutes ▪ Makes 4 servings**

▪ ▪ ▪

½ cup chopped onion

¼ cup water

6 smoked tomatoes, peeled, seeded, and chopped (page 26)

1 tablespoon minced garlic

⅛ teaspoon dried chili flakes

¼ teaspoon chili powder

¼ teaspoon ground cumin

3 cups vegetable broth

6 ounces fresh spinach, washed well, stemmed, and chopped

½ teaspoon salt

¼ teaspoon freshly ground black pepper

6 blue corn tortilla chips, for garnish

1. In a medium skillet, cook the onion and water over medium heat until the onion is tender. Add the tomatoes, garlic, chili flakes, chili powder, cumin, and broth and bring to a simmer.

2. Place the mixture in a blender or food processor and puree, in batches, but leave some texture.

3. Return the mixture to the pot. Add the spinach, salt, and pepper, and cook until the spinach is tender.

4. Serve in individual bowls with a tortilla chip floated on the top.

# ENTRÉES
## The Main Act

■ ■ ■

When I encounter nonvegetarians, I am often asked what I eat as my main course. It seems many people have a hard time getting their mind around the concept that you can have a satisfying entrée entirely from the plant world. It's all in the way we look at things. In truth, I can barely recall the days when I ate a plate of pork chops, potatoes, and green beans for dinner. Now, a Savory Winter Vegetable Strudel or Tuscan Melanzane will suffice, all by itself.

If we go back a bit in history we see that the hot, multi-course meal is something of a new practice. Many people's bodies do not respond well to having too many different foods tossed into the furnace. The result is often heartburn, bowel troubles, upset stomach, lethargy, and weight gain. More attention has been brought to this subject through knowledge of food combining. Although I am not strict about food combining by any means, I do follow the simple premise that one satisfying dish per meal, with perhaps a small accompaniment, leaves me feeling satisfied and energized. On the rare occasion when I eat a large, multi-course meal, I feel overtaxed and fatigued. At least for me, a good entrée goes a long way at the table. Obviously, the feelings I've just shared are for those of a healthy, active, middle-age woman. For those still in their growth years, as well as those who are extremely active physically or those who have a high metabolic rate, the picture changes as more calories are needed.

As modern medicine and science attempt to create a standardized template as to how we should feed ourselves, perhaps the only agreed-upon message is that humans have a need for fresh produce. There is little argument that the world of fruits, vegetables, legumes, seeds, and nuts offers a wealth of nutritional support for the body. In addition, what they offer cannot be replaced by manufactured foods. The vitamins, minerals, enzymes, fiber, and phytonutrients are not the same once altered.

In the following pages, you will find hearty, nutritious, and wonderful-tasting entrées that will surely add a bounty of nutrients to your daily food intake.

■ ■ ■

# Jerk-Style Black Beans

*Throughout the Caribbean, you'll find little stands where the owners proudly feature their version of steamy jerk dishes, usually pork or chicken. The tradition of jerk is said to date back to the seventeenth century, when fugitive African slaves brought their tradition of slow cooking together with the natives' cultivation and use of hot and aromatic spices to create this unique spice blend. Jerk comes in both a sauce form and dry spice blend. While jerk recipes are often closely guarded secrets of each cook in the Caribbean, there are some basic ingredients common to most jerk sauces and spice blends: cinnamon, nutmeg, black pepper, allspice, salt, herbs, brown sugar, garlic, and onion. Oil and vinegar are added to the sauce version.*

**Preparation Time: 15 minutes ▪ Cooking Time: 20 minutes ▪ Makes 4 to 6 servings**

1 medium onion, chopped

¼ cup water

1 green bell pepper, chopped

1 red bell pepper, chopped

2 (15-ounce) cans black beans, rinsed and drained

2 cups chopped fresh or canned tomatoes

2 teaspoons Jamaican jerk spice

1 teaspoon freshly grated or ground ginger

Salt, to taste

1. In a skillet over medium heat, cook the onion in the water, stirring, until softened, about 5 minutes.

2. Add the green and red bell peppers and cook, stirring, about 5 minutes, until tender.

3. Add the beans, tomatoes, jerk spice, ginger, and salt. Bring to a simmer, reduce the heat to low, and simmer for 15 minutes. Serve hot.

# Mu Shu Vegetables

Mu shu is a popular dim sum dish that is served unassembled and consists of delicate crepes and a choice of filling. Although classically made with meat of some kind, my vegetarian version of mu shu is a worthy competitor, bursting with the favorite flavors of Asia—garden-fresh vegetables adorned with garlic, ginger, hot pepper oil, and Szechwan sauce.

**Preparation Time: 30 minutes ▪ Cooking Time: 15 minutes ▪ Makes 4 to 6 servings**

2 leeks (white parts only), cut into fine strips

1 red bell pepper, cut into fine strips

2 Chinese eggplants, cut into fine strips

¼ cup water

2 sun-dried tomatoes, reconstituted in boiling water for 15 minutes and cut into fine strips

1 tablespoon minced garlic

1 tablespoon grated fresh ginger

4 tablespoons soy sauce

2 tablespoons balsamic vinegar

2 tablespoons hot pepper oil

2 tablespoons Szechwan-type sauce

Salt, to taste

1 cup sliced fresh basil

3 green onions (white and green parts), julienned, for garnish

Crepes (page 97)

1. In a skillet, cook the leeks, bell pepper, and eggplants in the water over medium-high heat, stirring, until tender, 8 to 10 minutes.

2. Add the sun-dried tomatoes, garlic, ginger, soy sauce, vinegar, hot pepper oil, and Szechwan sauce. Cook, stirring, 1 to 2 minutes until the vegetables are infused with the seasonings. Add salt, if needed.

3. Add the basil just before serving.

4. Serve the vegetables with a little of the green onions, rolled up in the crepes.

# Crepes

*Use these crepes for wrapping Mu Shu Vegetables (page 96) or other vegetable combinations. The crepes can be made ahead and stored in the refrigerator with waxed paper between each crepe to prevent them from sticking together.*

**Preparation Time: 10 minutes** ▪
**Cooking Time: 20 minutes** ▪ **Makes 6 to 8 crepes**

▪ ▪ ▪

> ¾ **cup all-purpose flour**
> ½ **teaspoon salt**
> 1 **teaspoon baking powder**
> 2 **large eggs, lightly beaten**
> ⅔ **cup milk**
> ⅓ **cup water**
> 1 **teaspoon vegetable oil per crepe for cooking**

1. Into a bowl, sift together the flour, salt, and baking powder. Make a well in the dry ingredients. Pour in the eggs, milk, and water. Mix together, but do not overblend. A few lumps are fine.

2. Heat an 8-inch skillet or crepe pan over medium-high heat. Add 1 teaspoon oil and tip the skillet to coat the bottom of the pan. Ladle 2 to 3

## What's Brewing in China

With the turn of the millennium, China became the largest beer-brewing nation in the world. Because the country had no brewing tradition, China relied on foreign expertise in the developmental phases of the industry. Among the influences were the Germans at Tsingtao and the Russians at Harbin. Recent estimates put the number of breweries in China at around 850, which does not account for local unregistered breweries. And with the Chinese fiercely loyal to their local beer, it's the local town breweries that account for the lion's share of the beer business.

As with any other beer-producing country, it would be difficult to give a quick definition of Chinese beer. It ranges from a bright pineapple-flavored lager called Sweet China, to Emperor's Gold Beer, which leaves a slightly molasses aftertaste, to a dark lager called Guangminpai.

tablespoons batter into the pan. Quickly tilt the pan to cover the bottom with batter, spreading the batter with a plastic spatula if necessary. You will need to work fast, as the batter sets up very quickly.

3. Cook until browned on the bottom, then turn over to brown the other side. Turn the crepe out on to a plate. Repeat until all the batter is used, adding 1 teaspoon oil to the skillet between crepes.

# *foo yong* · · · ·

## *Egg Foo Yong*

*Many cultures have their version of an omelet or frittata, and this is the Chinese version. Unlike the Egg Foo Yong brought home in little white cartons from the neighborhood Chinese restaurant, you will notice that there is no sauce with these patties. I find that a sauce not only adds a large amount of sodium to an Egg Foo Yong dish, but also detracts from the wonderful flavor of these egg and vegetable patties.*

**Preparation Time: 30 minutes ▪ Cooking Time: 10 minutes ▪ Makes 8 patties**
▪ ▪ ▪

> 8 ounces mushrooms, sliced
>
> 1 carrot, thinly sliced
>
> ½ cup chopped green onions (green and white parts), chopped
>
> 1 cup vegetable broth
>
> 1 generous teaspoon seasoning salt
>
> ½ teaspoon chili flakes (optional)
>
> 4 teaspoons onion powder
>
> 1 teaspoon garlic powder
>
> ½ teaspoon sesame oil
>
> 8 ounces fresh bean sprouts
>
> 3 tablespoons all-purpose flour
>
> 4 large eggs, lightly beaten
>
> 1 teaspoon butter per patty, for cooking

1. In a pot, bring the mushrooms, carrot, onions, and broth to a boil over medium-high heat. Reduce the heat and simmer until the vegetables are slightly tender and the liquid has evaporated.

2. Add the seasoning salt, chili flakes (if using), onion powder, garlic powder, and sesame oil, and stir.

3. Add the sprouts and toss quickly for 30 to 40 seconds, until the sprouts just begin to wilt. Remove from the heat and transfer to a bowl.

4. Add the flour to the bowl, and stir until the vegetables are coated. Stir in the eggs.

5. Heat a skillet over medium heat. Add 1 teaspoon butter to coat the bottom of the pan. Spoon ⅓ cup egg mixture into the skillet and cook until golden brown on both sides, turning once. Remove the cooked patty to a plate. Add 1 teaspoon butter to the skillet and repeat until all the egg mixture is cooked.

## All the Tea in China

China still produces the widest array of the world's finest teas, with much of the production taking place as it always has—by hand. Eighty percent of the tea cultivated is green tea used for domestic consumption. In the West, however, we generally associate Chinese cuisine with oolong and black teas, as these teas have been more prevalent in our societies. One of the favorites is oolong tea, which is produced from partially fermented leaves. This process creates teas with a flavor, color, and aroma that fall somewhere between green tea and black tea. Oolong tea is often scented with various blossoms and spices such as jasmine or citrus peel. For purposes of preparing a meal, we'll focus on this type of tea, as the world of tea is so rich entire volumes have been written on single varieties.

*Brewing Hints for Oolong Tea*
Brew 1 teaspoon tea in 1 cup water that has not quite reached the boiling point. Infuse for 5 to 7 minutes for the full flavor. Some of the fuller-flavored, amber-colored oolong teas can be served with milk and sugar if you prefer. Other lighter and crisper oolongs are best served alone.

One of the most special oolong teas is called Ti Kwan Yin, which means the Iron Goddess of Mercy. This is one of the most sought-after teas in China, so you should expect to pay a premium if you can find it. I would suggest going online if you want to explore more of the tea world.

# Savory Winter Vegetable Strudel

*This steamy, golden strudel is a dish I trot out at winter pot-luck dinners, which are frequent in my small town. The men rave about it, and the women ask for the recipe. The secret is in buying the freshest leeks, cauliflower, broccoli, and turnips available, preferably organic. You will be surprised at what a difference it makes in the overall sweetness and taste of this wonderful winter entrée. The other little twist to this savory strudel is the use of mustard in the low-fat egg mixture that binds the vegetables together.*

**Preparation Time: 35 minutes ▪ Cooking Time: 20 minutes ▪ Makes 6 servings**

▪ ▪ ▪

2 leeks (white parts only), sliced

1 large onion, sliced

About 1 cup vegetable broth or water

Seasoning salt, to taste

½ head cauliflower, chopped

1 turnip, peeled and diced

1 medium crown broccoli, cut into small florets

⅛ to ¼ teaspoon freshly ground black pepper

2 teaspoons aged balsamic vinegar

1 sheet (½ [17.3-ounce] package) puff pastry, thawed

2 eggs or ½ cup egg substitute

½ cup fat-free evaporated milk

1 tablespoon prepared mustard

Pinch white pepper

Pinch nutmeg

½ cup freshly grated Parmesan cheese

1. Preheat the oven to 400F (205C).

2. Cook the leeks and onion in about 2 tablespoons broth in a large skillet until somewhat softened, 3 to 4 minutes. Season with seasoning salt and add water if mixture becomes too dry and sticks to the pan.

3. Add the cauliflower, turnip, broccoli, black pepper, balsamic vinegar, and more broth to the vegetable mixture and continue to cook until the vegetables are crisp-tender, 5 to 6 minutes. Add more broth or water if the vegetables begin to stick to the pan.

4. Cut off one-third of the puff pastry sheet and set aside. Line the bottom of a 9-inch-square baking dish with the larger piece of puff pastry. Bake for 6 minutes and remove from the oven.

5. Mix the eggs, milk, mustard, white pepper, and nutmeg together in a bowl. Set aside.

6. Arrange the vegetables over the baked puff pastry. Sprinkle the cheese over the vegetables. Pour the egg mixture over the vegetables and cheese and gently stir the cheese and vegetables until there's an even distribution of cheese throughout the dish.

7. Cut the remaining piece of puff pastry into strips and lay the strips across the top of the vegetables.

8. Bake for 20 minutes, until pastry is brown. Serve hot.

# Root Vegetables with Sherry

*It takes a strong root to grow through the solid, cold soil and sustain life above. The earthiest of earth's bounty, this recipe is deeply rooted (pun intended) in the tradition of Eastern European cuisine. This panoply of root vegetables is augmented with the flavors of sherry and white pepper to create as healthful a dish as can be found in the dead of winter.*

**Preparation Time: 30 minutes ▪ Cooking Time: 20 to 30 minutes ▪ Makes 4 to 6 servings**

▪ ▪ ▪

1½ pounds assorted root vegetables such as turnips, carrots, rutabaga, celery root, and parsnips, peeled

1 large onion, sliced vertically from stem to root end

About ½ cup water or vegetable broth

2 tablespoons extra-virgin olive oil

¼ cup dry sherry

1 teaspoon salt

¼ teaspoon white pepper, or to taste

1. If using parsnips, remove the fibrous core that runs down the center. To do this, cut the parsnip into quarters and, using a paring knife, cut out the core. Cut all root vegetables into sticks of fairly equal thickness and length.

2. Cook the onion in ½ cup water in a large skillet over medium-high heat until the onion is softened and most of the water has evaporated. Add the olive oil, sherry, root vegetables, salt, and white pepper.

3. Cover the skillet and cook over medium-low heat for about 20 minutes, until the vegetables are tender, adding a little vegetable broth or water if the mixture becomes too dry before the vegetables have softened. Check for seasoning and serve hot.

# *Grilled Vegetables with Navy Bean Sauce*

*Low in fat, yet creamy and full-tasting, bean sauces are a wonderful replacement for the traditional French cream sauces. In this dish, the flavor is given a further boost by the smoky flavor imparted from the grilled summer vegetables. The following list of vegetables is only a suggestion, as just about any vegetable will work well with this sauce and the grill. After all, there's no such thing as a bad grilled vegetable!*

**Preparation Time: 30 minutes ▪ Cooking Time: 10 minutes ▪ Makes 4 to 6 servings**

▪ ▪ ▪

1 cup cooked white beans

½ cup vegetable broth, plus ½ cup for puree

2 cloves garlic, chopped

¼ cup diced onion

¼ cup chopped roasted red bell pepper (page 87)

¼ tablespoon ground cumin

Salt and freshly ground black pepper, to taste

2 tablespoons extra-virgin olive oil

12 drops chili oil, or a dash of cayenne (optional)

6 squash, such as zucchini, crookneck, or summer squash, cut into ¼-inch-thick slices

Freshly grated hard cheese, such as Parmesan, Asiago, or Grana Padano

1. In a medium saucepan, combine the beans, ½ cup broth, garlic, onion, bell pepper, cumin, salt, black pepper, and olive oil. Bring to a boil and cook for 8 to 10 minutes.

2. Stir in the chili oil (if using).

3. Place the mixture into a blender and puree until smooth, adding enough broth for the desired consistency.

4. Brush the squash with olive oil, and season with salt and pepper. Grill on both sides until the slices are lightly charred. Transfer the squash to a serving dish, and spoon the sauce over the squash.

5. Sprinkle with grated cheese. Serve hot.

# Winter Vegetables with Dates

*This dish is the inspiration of French chef Theirry Rauturau, who tantalizes all his clients at Rover's in Seattle with his splendid fare. I featured him on one of my cooking programs, and this is the creation* du jour *he shared with the audience. It has been amended slightly to meet my personal preferences, but the concept remains intact. Serve with rice or a risotto dish.*

**Preparation Time: 30 minutes** ▪ **Cooking Time: 10 minutes** ▪ **Makes 4 to 6 servings**

▪ ▪ ▪

2 cups vegetable broth

1 onion, minced

Bouquet garni (page 107, optional)

2 small turnips, peeled and cut into ⅓-inch strips

2 small rutabagas, peeled and cut into ⅓-inch strips

4 teaspoons butter or olive oil

2 cups thinly sliced leeks (white parts only)

2 cups sliced mushrooms

Hearty splash of sherry

4 teaspoons chopped fresh oregano

½ cup chopped, pitted fresh dates

1. In a saucepan, simmer 1 cup of the vegetable broth, onion, and bouquet garni (if using) for 5 minutes, until the onion is tender. Strain the onion and herbs out and set the broth aside.

2. In a separate saucepan, simmer the turnips and rutabagas in another ½ cup broth over medium heat for 4 to 5 minutes, until the vegetables are tender.

3. In a skillet, heat the butter and the remaining ½ cup vegetable broth over medium-high heat. Add the leeks, mushrooms, and sherry. Cook for 2 to 3 minutes.

4. Add the root vegetables, oregano, and dates to the mushroom mixture, and toss to combine.

5. Serve hot.

## Making Your Own Bouquet Garni

Bouquet garni is nothing more than a small bunch of herbs in bondage. The most common combination is bay leaves, thyme, marjoram, and parsley. The herbs are placed in small muslin bags, which can be found in gourmet shops, or rolled into bundles. To make your own bundles, cut an 8-inch-square piece of cheesecloth, place the herbs toward one end, and roll it up, folding the loose ends of cheesecloth in toward the center. Take some thin cotton twine and tie off each end so the herbs cannot escape during cooking.

Fresh herbs provide the best flavor when available, but use them soon after rolling them, as they will mildew if stored. Another option is to use your own dried-whole herbs. Or you can use dried store-bought herbs as long as they are not ground to a powder form. Just make the bundle smaller for these dried herbs.

The purpose for using bouquet garni rather than the loose herbs in a dish is to infuse the stocks or sauces with just a hint of the herbal flavor without overwhelming it. It also keeps the sauce "clean" looking and makes the herbs easier to remove.

# Pecan Baked Zucchini

*The French have a love affair with their vegetables, zucchini being one of the national favorites. This simple baked zucchini dish gets its crunch and flavor from sautéed shallots and pecans, though hazelnuts would work nicely as well.*

*For the fullest flavor, find garden-fresh zucchini if you can, or buy organic.*

**Preparation Time: 20 minutes** ▪ **Cooking Time: 20 minutes** ▪ **Makes 4 servings**

2 shallots, finely minced

1½ tablespoons butter

4 zucchini, sliced in half lengthwise, ends removed, scored with 4 to 5 small diagonal cuts into the pulp

Pinch nutmeg, preferably freshly grated

Salt and freshly ground black pepper, to taste

2 to 3 tablespoons toasted bread crumbs or saltine cracker crumbs

¼ cup pecan meal (see Note below)

Extra-virgin olive oil

¼ cup freshly grated Parmesan cheese

1. Preheat the oven to 350F (190C). In a small skillet, cook the shallots and butter over medium heat until the shallots are softened.

2. Place the zucchini halves, cut side up, on a baking sheet. Spoon the shallots over the top of each half. Sprinkle each with nutmeg, salt, and pepper.

3. Combine the bread crumbs and pecan meal in a small bowl. Sprinkle a generous layer onto each zucchini half.

4. Lightly drizzle olive oil on top of the crumbs. Sprinkle with the cheese.

5. Bake for 15 to 17 minutes, until hot. Set the oven to broil. Broil until the top is golden and crispy. Serve hot.

**Note:** Grind crackers or pecans in a food processor to make crumbs or meal.

# Nutmeg

Nutmeg was one of the proverbial dangling carrots that drove Columbus forward in his search for the East Indies and its spices. Native to the Spice Islands, nutmeg was popular in much of the world from the fifteenth to the nineteenth century.

Nutmeg is a seed at the center of the fruit of the nutmeg tree, a tropical evergreen. When the fruit is split open, it reveals the seed, which is surrounded by a lacy membrane. When that lacy membrane is dried and ground, it becomes the spice called mace. The egg-shaped nutmeg seed is hard and about one inch in length. Its sweet, delicate, warming flavor makes it ideal to pair with any dairy dish as well as vegetables such as spinach, squash, and potatoes. It is often used in ricotta-filled ravioli and in many Middle Eastern dishes.

As versatile as it is, it is well worth investing in a small nutmeg grater, as the flavor of freshly ground nutmeg is superior to pre-ground nutmeg. Though the nutmeg seed is hard, it is surprisingly easy to grate by hand. I prefer a small, flat, metal grater. Nutmeg grinders, which resemble pepper grinders, are also available. Once you begin using freshly ground nutmeg you'll be looking for opportunities to use it more! Don't go overboard, however, as nutmeg is very strong flavored and it can be a hallucinogenic—that is *if* you were to eat a couple whole seeds!

# Orzo with Fava Beans and Tomatoes

*At first glance, orzo appears to be off-colored grains of rice. Although the Italian translation for orzo means "barley," it is, in fact, semolina formed into tiny rice-shaped dried pasta. Orzo is wonderful in soups and is often used as a substitute for rice in hearty entrées and side dishes like the following.*

**Preparation time: I hour  ▪  Cooking Time: 20 minutes  ▪  Makes 6 servings**

▪ ▪ ▪

1 pound orzo

1 red bell pepper, chopped

½ cup water

2 cups fresh fava beans, or 1 (19-ounce) can fava beans

2 tablespoons minced garlic

4 tablespoons extra-virgin olive oil

3 cups peeled, seeded, fresh or canned tomatoes

2 tablespoons chopped fresh oregano

Salt and freshly ground black pepper, to taste

¼ cup grated myzythra cheese (Greek sheep milk cheese)

1. In a saucepan, cook the orzo in boiling salted water following the package instructions.

2. While the orzo is cooking, cook the red bell pepper in the water over medium heat until the water mostly evaporates and the bell pepper is tender.

3. If you are using fresh fava beans, remove the beans from the pods. Blanch the fava beans in boiling water for about 5 minutes. Drain and rinse them in cold water. Peel the outer membranes off the beans. Steam them, covered, with a little water for about 7 minutes, until they are tender.

4. Add the fava beans, garlic, and 1 tablespoon olive oil to the bell pepper. Cook for 3 to 4 minutes over medium heat.

5. Drain the orzo and drizzle it with 1 tablespoon olive oil to keep it from sticking together. Add the tomatoes, oregano, and the remaining 2 tablespoons olive oil to the fava bean mixture.

6. Season with salt and pepper. Heat until hot.

7. Pour the fava bean mixture over the orzo and toss to combine. Sprinkle each serving with a little cheese. Serve hot.

## Fava Beans

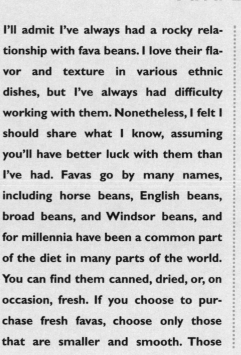

I'll admit I've always had a rocky relationship with fava beans. I love their flavor and texture in various ethnic dishes, but I've always had difficulty working with them. Nonetheless, I felt I should share what I know, assuming you'll have better luck with them than I've had. Favas go by many names, including horse beans, English beans, broad beans, and Windsor beans, and for millennia have been a common part of the diet in many parts of the world. You can find them canned, dried, or, on occasion, fresh. If you choose to purchase fresh favas, choose only those that are smaller and smooth. Those that are bulging have a tougher and bitter bean inside. The beans must be removed from the pods, boiled for about 5 minutes, cooled in ice water, and the outer skin of each individual bean removed and discarded. The pod is edible only if it is very immature, as they become tough and stringy as they reach maturity. The Romans enjoyed eating the very young and tender fava with slices of pecorino, a sheep milk cheese that has become very popular in recent years in the United States.

As for dried favas, don't use salt in the water when you boil them. Season the beans with salt *after* they are tender.

*chard*

## Lentil Stew with Chard

*The little lens-shaped lentil is a powerhouse of nutrition, which is why it is so widely used throughout the cuisines of the Mediterranean. There are four main varieties of lentils available. The European lentil, with a grayish-brown exterior is the most common and is found in most supermarkets. The Egyptian red lentil, which is smaller, and the yellow lentil are generally found in Middle Eastern or East Indian specialty shops or health food stores. The small, dark-green French lentil will also work well in this dish.*

**Preparation Time: 20 minutes • Cooking Time: 60 minutes • Makes 6 servings**

■ ■ ■

1 medium onion, diced

3 cloves garlic, minced

6 cups water or vegetable broth

4 ounces dried lentils

1 stalk celery, finely chopped

1/2 teaspoon curry powder

1/4 teaspoon ground cumin

15-ounce canned chopped tomatoes

2 to 3 tablespoons extra-virgin olive oil (optional)

Salt, to taste

3 cups chopped chard leaves, stems removed

1. In a large skillet, cook the onion, garlic, and water over medium-high heat for 3 to 5 minutes, until the onion is softened.

2. Add all the other ingredients except the chard. Simmer, covered, for about 45 minutes, adding small amounts of water during the cooking if needed.

3. Add the chard and simmer about 15 minutes, until the lentils are soft. Serve hot.

■ ■ ■

# *Moussaka*

*Moussaka is one of the most popular entrées in Greek cuisine. Although it is traditionally made with eggplant and ground lamb or beef, it is simple to create a delectable vegetarian version. In our adaptation of moussaka, we substitute zucchini, peppers, and onion for the meat. Sweet and savory spices give it the legs to dance on your tongue.*

**Preparation Time: I hour ■ Cooking Time: 45 minutes ■ Makes 6 servings**

■ ■ ■

2 globe eggplants, sliced

Salt and freshly ground black pepper, to taste

Extra-virgin olive oil

1 large onion, chopped

1 red bell pepper, chopped

1 yellow bell pepper, chopped

3 tablespoons water

3 tablespoons minced garlic

6 medium zucchini, sliced

⅛ teaspoon ground allspice

⅛ teaspoon ground cinnamon

1½ teaspoons herbes de Provence

2 (28-ounce) cans Italian-style tomatoes

2 tablespoons sun-dried tomato pesto

1 cup crumbled feta cheese

Classic Béchamel Sauce (page 115)

⅓ cup freshly grated Parmesan cheese

1. Lay the eggplants on baking sheets in a single layer. Salt the pieces, brush them lightly with olive oil on each side, and bake at 400F (205C) for 15 to 20 minutes, until tender, but still holding its shape. Reduce oven temperature to 350F (180C).

2. In a medium skillet, simmer the onion, red and yellow bell peppers, and water over medium heat for 5 to 7 minutes, until the onion is softened. Add the garlic, zucchini, allspice, cinnamon, and herbes de Provence. Cook for 3 minutes, until the zucchini is tender.

3. Drain and chop the tomatoes. Add the tomatoes and tomato pesto to the onion mixture and simmer for 1 to 2 minutes. Season with salt and pepper.

4. Lightly brush a baking dish with olive oil. Place a layer of eggplant, followed by a layer of the tomato-vegetable sauce, then a layer of feta. Repeat the layering until the eggplant, half the feta cheese, and sauce are used up.

5. Prepare the Béchamel Sauce, and stir in the Parmesan cheese. Pour the sauce evenly over the top of the moussaka. Sprinkle the remaining crumbled feta cheese on top and bake at 350F for about 45 minutes, until bubbling and the top is brown. Remove from the oven and let sit for about 15 minutes before serving.

# Classic Béchamel Sauce

*Béchamel is the basic white sauce used for thickening and as a topping for casseroles.*

**Preparation Time: 5 minutes** ▪ **Cooking Time: 6 minutes** ▪ **Makes 1 ½ cups**

▪ ▪ ▪

> 3 tablespoons butter
> 3 tablespoons all-purpose flour
> 1½ cups whole milk or plain almond milk
> Salt and white pepper, to taste

1. In a small saucepan, melt the butter over medium heat. Gradually add the flour, stirring, to make a paste.

2. Slowly stir in the milk and season with salt and white pepper. Cook, stirring constantly, until the sauce thickens.

# Madras Vegetables with Rice

*There has always been much debate and misunderstanding as to what constitutes a curry dish. If you speak to an Indian cook, they will tell you it is a process of reducing tomatoes, onions, garlic, and spices to a paste to be used as the flavoring base of a dish. It is not a dish that utilizes curry powder. This is why, although this dish may taste like what you know as a curry dish, I have not called it such.*

**Preparation Time: 45 minutes** ▪ **Cooking Time: 20 minutes** ▪ **Makes 4 to 6 servings**

▪ ▪ ▪

2 cups water

2 cups brown basmati rice

Salt

1 tablespoon Madras curry powder

1 tablespoon extra-virgin olive oil

2 cups vegetable broth

2 carrots, peeled and cut into thin strips

1 small head broccoli, florets only

1 small head cauliflower, cored and cut into florets

2 tablespoons peanut oil

1 medium onion, thinly sliced

1 tablespoon minced garlic

Chutney (optional)

1. In a medium saucepan, bring the water to a boil. Add the rice and a dash of salt. Cover the pan, reduce the heat to low, and simmer for 20 to 30 minutes, until the rice reaches the desired consistency.

2. In a small skillet, warm the curry powder and olive oil over low heat, watching carefully so that it does not burn. You only want to warm it to release its flavors. Add the broth and simmer for 20 to 30 minutes, until the liquid reduces by about one-third.

3. Bring a pot of water to boil and boil the carrots, broccoli, and cauliflower until they are crisp-tender but not completely cooked. Drain and set aside.

4. Heat a large skillet over high heat. Add the peanut oil and onion. Cook until the onion is softened, stirring constantly with a spatula so it doesn't burn. Add the garlic and cook for about 30 seconds. Add the carrots, broccoli, cauliflower, and reduced broth. Cook until the vegetables are tender.

5. Serve over the basmati rice with chutney (if using).

*india* **India House Frittata**

■ ■ ■

Although frittatas are not native to Indian cuisine, I like to use eggs as a means of adding some extra protein and nutrients to the diet. So here, we are offering an eclectic interpretation of what would be an Indian frittata spiked with the traditional flavors of garam masala, cayenne, onion, and garlic.

**Preparation Time: 20 minutes ▪ Cooking Time: 20 minutes ▪ Makes 4 to 6 servings**

■ ■ ■

1½ cups chopped onions

3 cloves garlic, chopped

1 cup vegetable broth

1½ cups chopped yellow or green pattypan squash

2 tablespoons sherry

1 to 2 tablespoons extra-virgin olive oil

2 teaspoons Garam Masala (page 120), or purchased

Pinch cayenne pepper

Salt, to taste

2 teaspoons butter or olive oil, for cooking

4 eggs, lightly beaten, or 1 cup egg substitute

3 ounces Asiago or aged Gouda cheese, finely grated

Chopped fresh parsley, for garnish

Plain yogurt

1. Preheat the oven to 350F (180C). Simmer the onions, garlic, and broth in a skillet over medium heat until the onions become transparent.

2. Add the squash and cook for 2 minutes, stirring frequently. Add the sherry, olive oil, Garam Masala, cayenne, and salt. Cook for 1 minute. Remove from the heat.

3. Place the butter in an 8-inch oven-safe skillet or pie pan and heat on the stovetop over medium heat until the butter melts. Spread the vegetables evenly in the skillet. Gently pour the eggs over the vegetables. Sprinkle two-thirds of the cheese into the mixture, gently stirring with a fork. Sprinkle the remaining cheese on top.

4. Place the skillet in the oven and bake for 15 to 20 minutes. Remove from the oven and garnish with the parsley. Serve with plain yogurt on the side.

# *masala*

## *Garam Masala*

*There are several different recipes for making garam masala. Garam means "warm," and masala means "spices." Not all recipes call for garam masala, yet it can be added to almost any north Indian curry, in small amounts. Almost every region in India has its own spice mixture with differing names. Although garam masala tends to have a sweetness to it, other regional spice mixtures may be more pungent or hot and spicy. And although garam masala is a powdered mixture, others may be pastes, incorporating ground whole red chilies and oil or vinegar.*

*All the whole spices listed below are available from any Indian grocer. While roasting the whole spices in a skillet, the aroma will be quite strong and will quickly spread throughout your home. Therefore, ensure that you open/close some windows depending on how aromatic you would like your home to be. The following recipe is from the acclaimed Vancouver, B.C., restaurant Vij's.*

**Preparation Time: 10 minutes ∎ Cooking Time: 5 to 10 minutes ∎ Makes ¾ cup**

∎ ∎ ∎

> **1 heaping teaspoon whole cloves**
>
> **1½ teaspoons black cardamom seeds (from 10 pods)**
>
> **6 heaping tablespoons whole cumin seeds**
>
> **1 level tablespoon chopped or finely broken cinnamon sticks**
>
> **¼ teaspoon powdered mace**
>
> **¼ teaspoon freshly grated nutmeg**

1. In a dry heavy iron skillet, heat the cloves, cardamom seeds, cumin seeds, and cinnamon sticks over medium to high heat, stirring constantly to prevent burning.

2. When the cumin seeds change to a darker shade of brown (not a dark brown), remove the pan from the heat and let it cool.

3. Once cooled, add the mace and nutmeg and grind the spices in a spice or coffee grinder.

**Note:** Store in an airtight jar for up to three months. Garam masala also makes a wonderful gift for more adventurous home chefs.

# Tuscan Melanzane

*Italian comfort food with a piquant twist is how I would categorize this layered eggplant dish. Although it is prepared in a style similar to lasagna, it has none of the refined carbohydrates from pasta, but all the wonderful flavors of the Mediterranean.*

**Preparation Time: 30 minutes** ▪ **Cooking Time: 20 minutes** ▪ **Makes 4 servings**

1 medium to large globe eggplant, peeled and sliced into 1/3-inch slices

Olive oil, for brushing

Salt and freshly ground black pepper, to taste

3 ounces Havarti cheese, grated

1 1/2 ounces feta cheese, crumbled

2 red bell peppers, roasted, peeled, and cut into 1/2-inch strips (page 87)

2/3 cup prepared pasta sauce

1 to 2 teaspoons capers, drained

Herbes de Provence, to taste

1 ounce Parmesan cheese, grated

1. Preheat the oven to broil. Place the eggplant slices on a baking sheet in a single layer. Lightly brush the eggplant slices on each side with olive oil and season with salt and pepper.

2. Broil the eggplant for 4 to 5 minutes. Reduce oven temperature to 375F (190C).

3. Mix the Havarti and feta cheeses together in a bowl.

4. Layer the ingredients in an 8-inch-square baking dish in the following order: half the eggplant slices, half the bell peppers, 1/3 cup of the pasta sauce, all the capers, a generous sprinkling of herbes de Provence, and all the cheese mixture. Repeat with the remaining eggplant, bell peppers, and pasta sauce. Top with the Parmesan cheese.

5. Bake for about 10 minutes, until the cheese melts.

# *gnocchi...* ▪▪▪

## *Ricotta Gnocchi*

*This pillowy gnocchi is inspired by the famed dish served at Picholine in New York City. Being a new diner, I asked the waiter to point me toward the house specialty. Without a blink he suggested I try the gnocchi. I did, and was sent directly to heaven! I asked if the chef/owner would be willing to join me on my cooking program and share the recipe. (How else would I get these top-notch chefs to share their secrets?!) Chef/owner Terrance Brennan agreed to join me and allowed me to share his famed recipe with you, with slight revisions to compensate for hard-to-find ingredients. Enjoy!*

**Preparation Time: 20 minutes ▪ Cooking Time: 10 minutes ▪ Makes 6 servings**
▪ ▪ ▪

> **15-ounce container ricotta cheese**
>
> **2 ounces chevre**
>
> **½ teaspoon freshly grated nutmeg**
>
> **⅓ cup freshly grated hard cheese such as Parmesan, Grana Padano, or Asiago**
>
> **¼ teaspoon salt**
>
> **Pinch cayenne pepper**
>
> **¾ cup unbleached white flour**
>
> **Olive oil, to drizzle**
>
> **Mushroom Ragout (page 124), olive oil, or butter, to serve**

1. In a bowl, mix together the ricotta, chevre, nutmeg, cheese, salt, and cayenne until smooth.

2. Gently stir in the flour, a small amount at a time.

3. On a well-floured surface, with floured hands, pinch off a handful of the dough and begin rolling it out like a log into a ½-inch-diameter rope. Cut the rope, diagonally, into 1-inch lengths. Press a small well into the center of each piece and place the pieces on a platter. Repeat the process until all the dough is gone.

4. Have ready a large bowl filled with ice water. Bring a large pot of salted water to a boil. Drop the gnocchi into the salted water (it works best if not more than 12 gnocchi are cooked at a time). Cook only until the pieces begin to float to the top of the water. Quickly remove the gnocchi from the water with a slotted spoon and drop them in the ice water for a few minutes to stop the cooking. Remove the gnocchi from the ice water and place them onto a baking sheet. Drizzle with a little olive oil. The gnocchi are now ready to use or be stored. They will keep for a couple days in a tightly covered container in the refrigerator.

5. Before serving, drop the gnocchi into boiling salted water and cook for about 1 minute until they begin to float. Remove the gnocchi with a slotted spoon. Place them onto a serving dish and top with Mushroom Ragout.

# Mushroom Ragout

*The original reduced morel mushroom sauce served at Picholine has been replaced with this quicker version that makes the half-and-half optional for those on a fat-restricted diet.*

**Preparation Time: 15 minutes** ▪ **Cooking Time: 15 minutes** ▪ **Makes 4 to 6 servings**

2 cups vegetable broth

1 large onion, coarsely chopped

4 cloves garlic, minced

1 teaspoon Italian seasoning or herbes de Provence

2 tablespoons extra-virgin olive oil

1 pound mixture of mushrooms, any variety, sliced, if large

Salt and freshly ground black pepper, to taste

2 tablespoons cooking sherry

¼ cup half-and-half (optional)

1. In a large skillet, cook ½ cup of the vegetable broth, onion, garlic, and Italian seasoning over medium-high heat until the onion is softened, about 5 minutes.

2. Add the oil, mushrooms, salt, pepper, and sherry and cook for about 5 minutes, until the mushrooms are soft and only a small amount of the liquid remains.

3. Add the half-and-half, if using, and simmer 1 or 2 minutes, until the mixture reaches the consistency of a sauce.

4. Serve hot over gnocchi or pasta.

# Pappardelle Romano

There is something terribly sensuous about a broad, smooth, pappardelle noodle sliding over the tongue. This wide, flat noodle can be found in Italian markets and many gourmet shops. If the search for these lovely ribbons of pasta proves to be too arduous, you can use any other type of ribbon noodle available, such as fettuccine.

**Preparation Time: 30 minutes ▪ Cooking Time: 30 minutes ▪ Makes 4 to 6 servings**

▪ ▪ ▪

8 ounces wide pasta noodles

¼ cup extra-virgin olive oil

2 tomatoes, peeled and diced (see Note below)

⅓ cup chopped ripe olives

3 cloves garlic, minced

1 tablespoon capers, drained

Salt and freshly ground black pepper, to taste

½ bunch fresh spinach, washed and stemmed

⅓ cup freshly grated Parmesan cheese

1. Cook the pasta according to package directions and drain.

2. In a skillet, heat the olive oil over medium heat. Add the tomatoes, olives, garlic, capers, salt, and pepper. Cook for 3 to 4 minutes.

3. Add the spinach and cook until wilted, about 30 seconds.

4. Place the pasta on a serving platter. Ladle the vegetables over the pasta. Top with the Parmesan. Serve hot.

**Note:** To peel a tomato: Make a cross cut through the skin on the blossom end. Gently drop the tomato into boiling water for 30 to 60 seconds. Remove the tomato with a slotted spoon. Allow the tomato to cool and the skin should peel off easily with a knife.

# Pasta

In the United States, we tend to equate Italian pasta dishes with the thick, red sauces simmered for hours by an attentive Italian grandmother. In truth, many of the sauces you find at authentic Italian restaurants are made to order. Papparadelle Romano (page 125) is a good example of a pasta dish that comes together in 15 to 20 minutes.

While the water is reaching the boiling point and the pasta is cooking, the tomatoes are cut, garlic pressed, herbs torn, and spices lined up and ready to go. Once the cooking begins, it takes only minutes for the tomatoes to soften and for the flavors of the other ingredients to blend. The end result is a sauce that is not only full flavored, but also fresh and light.

This is, admittedly, a departure from the nostalgic sauces we may have been raised on, but once you begin to make your sauces to order, you may find yourself more willing to rattle those pots and pans when you have a yin for Italian. The beauty of fresh Italian pasta sauces is that there are no hard-and-fast rules. If you don't have any fresh tomatoes on hand, use canned tomatoes. If you have none of those, just press loads of garlic, drizzle olive oil over the top, and toss with the pasta. Add a little salt and freshly grated Parmesan cheese, and you have a simple but lovely pasta dish.

*Pasta Cooking Tips*

Unless you are on a strict sodium-free diet, always salt the water before boiling the pasta. You want to be careful not to overcook the pasta to a mushy texture. Instead, remove a strand of pasta intermittently and let it cool for a few seconds. When you bite into it, the pasta should have just a little firmness to the teeth.

As for rinsing the pasta, this depends on the dish you are making. If it is a hot pasta dish, don't rinse. When you rinse it, the starch is removed from the outside of the pasta. Leaving the starch on allows the pasta sauce to adhere to the strands better. Cold pasta dishes, such as pasta salads, are another matter. Here you do not want sticky strands, so it's better to rinse the pasta in cold water before putting the salad together.

# *Grilled Teriyaki Eggplant*

*The sweet and salty characteristic of teriyaki sauce makes it the perfect complement to a wide array of vegetable dishes. Eggplant and teriyaki is one of the more popular pairings at the Japanese table. What gives this version of eggplant teriyaki a more complex flavor is the smokiness imparted by pre-grilling the vegetables. And no one leaves the table hungry when this sweet and smoky eggplant dish is served over rice.*

**Preparation Time: 30 minutes ▪ Cooking Time: 20 minutes ▪ Makes 4 servings**

▪ ▪ ▪

> 1 large globe eggplant
> 1 large red bell pepper (see Note below)
> 1 bunch green onions, sliced lengthwise
> Salt and freshly ground black pepper, to taste
> 2 to 3 tablespoons peanut oil, plus extra for brushing
> ¼ cup Teriyaki Sauce (page 129)

1. Peel the eggplant and cut it into strips like french fries. Salt the strips and set aside for 20 minutes.

2. Cut the red bell pepper in half. Remove the veins and seeds. Grill the red pepper halves and green onions on the barbecue, indoor grill, or gas stove burners until they are charred. If none of these options are available, roast them in a hot oven for about 20 minutes. Place the peppers in a covered bowl and allow to cool. Peel off the skins. Cut the peppers into strips.

3. Rinse the salt from the eggplant and pat dry. Grill the eggplant using the same method, brushing with oil to prevent the eggplant from sticking to the grill or burners. Season both sides of the eggplant with salt and pepper during the grilling process.

4. In a large skillet over medium-high heat, combine the eggplant, peppers, peanut oil, and Teriyaki Sauce and quickly cook, stirring constantly, for about 30 seconds. Remove the skillet from the heat. Serve over rice.

**Note:** Prepared roasted red peppers in the jar can be used in place of fresh red bell peppers.

# Teriyaki Sauce

*This delectable sauce can be used as a marinade for a wide array of dishes and will keep for weeks in the refrigerator. Feel free to wave your creative wand over this recipe, as most marinades are a perfect way to express your own spicing preferences.*

**Preparation Time: 20 minutes • Cooking Time: 5 minutes • Makes 1¼ cups**

■ ■ ■

> 1 cup shoyu or soy sauce
>
> ⅓ cup honey
>
> 1½ tablespoons sesame seeds
>
> 1 tablespoon finely minced onion
>
> 2 cloves garlic, minced or pressed
>
> 8 to 10 drops sesame oil
>
> ¾ teaspoon finely grated fresh ginger

1. In a bowl, stir together the shoyu and honey until the honey is completely dissolved.

2. In a small, dry skillet, toast the sesame seeds over medium heat, stirring constantly, until they turn golden brown.

3. Combine the rest of the ingredients with the shoyu mixture. Refrigerate and use as desired.

### Japanese Rice

*Perhaps the most noticeable characteristic of Japanese rice is its stickiness. Second would be the straightforward flavor, unadorned by any seasonings, including salt. The method for making sticky rice is surprisingly simple. In the following recipe, I include shoyu sauce as the salt source for the rice to use before serving.*

**Preparation Time: 35 minutes ▪ Cooking Time: 30 minutes ▪ Makes 4 to 6 servings**

▪ ▪ ▪

**1 cup short-grain rice**
**1½ cups water**
**Shoyu sauce (optional)**

1. In a strainer, rinse the rice, place it in a bowl, and soak it in cold water for 30 minutes, then drain.

2. In a medium saucepan, bring the water to a boil. Add the rice and bring it quickly back to a boil.

3. Reduce the heat to low, cover, and simmer for 15 minutes.

4. Turn off the heat and let the rice stand for another 15 minutes. Season with shoyu (if using).

### Unfiltered Sake

It wasn't until recently that a friend shared with me the wonder of cold, unfiltered sake. My understanding of sake was limited to the clear, sharp-flavored, hot sake found in most Japanese restaurants. When my friend ordered unfiltered sake I had no idea what he was referring to. A pale, milky-colored beverage arrived. It had a sweet and nutty flavor with none of the sour or sharp tastes of the sake I had known.

Unfiltered sake is also a rice wine, but has not gone through the refining processes after fermentation. There are a wide variety of brands from which to choose, as well as a wide array of quality. I would suggest next time you are at your favorite Japanese restaurant, ask the waiter for a taste and see what you think.

# Eggplant and Chili Tacos

This is certainly not the type of taco you'd find at one of the thousands of outdoor taco stands throughout Mexico. Typically, you would pay the equivalent of 30 to 50 cents for a small corn tortilla filled with shredded or chopped beef, salsa, and other condiments. This has always been a bit of a problem for vegetarians, though some of the taco stands will fix a vegetarian version if they have refried beans on hand. We're going to bypass tradition entirely here and pile our taco shells full of this flavor-packed spicy eggplant-and-pepper filling!

**Preparation Time: 1 hour ▪ Cooking Time: 15 minutes ▪ Makes 12 tacos**

▪ ▪ ▪

> 2 cups peeled eggplant cubes
> Salt
> ½ cup finely chopped onion
> 1 cup water
> 1 tablespoon minced garlic
> 2 teaspoons chili powder
> 4-ounce can diced mild green chilies
> 1 red bell pepper, roasted, peeled, and chopped (page 87)
> 12 corn or flour tortillas
> 2 cups chopped fresh tomatoes
> 2 cups thinly sliced lettuce
> Fresh cilantro, washed and coarsely chopped (optional)
> 12-ounce package Mexican queso, thinly sliced, or shredded Cheddar or Monterey Jack cheese
> Salsa of your choice

1. Sprinkle the eggplant cubes with salt and set aside for 30 minutes, then blot them dry with a paper towel.

2. In a medium skillet, cook the onion and ½ cup of the water over medium-high heat until the onion is soft.

3. Add the eggplant, garlic, chili powder, and remaining ½ cup water to the onion. Simmer until the eggplant is tender. Add the chilies and roasted bell pepper. Cook until the water has evaporated. Season with salt.

4. Heat the tortillas by placing them in a nonstick fry pan on medium-high heat for 3 to 4 minutes each, or by wrapping them in aluminum foil and warming them in the oven, or by wrapping them in a damp paper towel and warming them in the microwave.

5. Spoon some of the eggplant mixture onto each tortilla. Top with the tomatoes, lettuce, cilantro (if using), cheese, and salsa. Serve warm.

*cheese*

# Three-Cheese Rellenos

*One of my lifelong Mexican favorites is chili rellenos. In our version, we expand on the traditional jack or queso filling by integrating a blend of cheeses, including a pepper jack for a little extra heat, along with cumin. The end result is light and highly flavorful.*

**Preparation Time: 45 minutes** ▪ **Cooking Time: 45 minutes** ▪ **Makes 4 servings**

▪ ▪ ▪

**SAUCE**
6 dried ancho or chipotle chilies
6 small dried red chilies
1 cup finely chopped onion
1 tablespoon olive oil
2 cups tomato puree
1 tablespoon minced garlic
1 teaspoon ground cumin
Salt and freshly ground black
    pepper, to taste

4 Anaheim or poblano chilies,
    or 7-ounce can whole chilies,
    drained

**FILLING**
1 cup grated Cheddar cheese
1 cup grated pepper jack cheese
½ cup ricotta cheese
1¼ teaspoons ground cumin

**BATTER**
3 eggs, separated
2 tablespoons all-purpose flour
Pinch salt
2 tablespoons milk

¼ cup mild vegetable oil, for
    cooking

1. To make the sauce: Place the ancho and red chilies on a baking sheet and toast them in the oven at 400F (205C) for 2 minutes. Remove from the oven and allow to cool. Crumble the chilies.

2. Cook the onion and oil in a medium skillet over medium-high heat until the onion is tender. Add the tomato puree, garlic, cumin, crumbled chilies, salt, and pepper. Turn the heat to low and simmer for 30 minutes. Place the sauce in a blender and puree until smooth.

3. Meanwhile, to prepare the chilies: If you are using fresh Anaheim chilies, blanch them in a large pot of boiling water for about 5 minutes, until tender. Remove the chilies, allow them to cool, and remove the skin. With a sharp knife, make a slit in the side of each chili. With a spoon, scoop out the seeds. Set aside.

4. If you are using canned chilies, make a slit in the side of each chili.

5. To make the filling: In a bowl, mix together the cheddar, pepper jack, and ricotta cheeses with the cumin. Gently spoon about 2 tablespoons of the filling into each chili.

6. To make the batter: In a bowl, beat the egg yolks and add the flour, salt, and milk. In a separate bowl, whip the egg whites until peaks form. Fold the egg whites into the batter.

7. To cook the rellenos: Heat a large skillet over medium-high heat. Add the oil and heat until just beginning to smoke. Dip each chili into the batter. Place the chili into the hot oil and cook on each side until the chili browns. Drain on paper towels.

8. Spoon the sauce over the cooked rellenos and serve.

# Chilies

Most home chefs have had some experience with stuffed peppers, most likely bell peppers, the mildest variety of what is commonly called peppers. Southwestern cuisine requires a bolder statement. Let's examine a few of the mild to medium heat chili peppers or chilies that can be used interchangeably in south-of-the-border dishes.

Anaheim chilies: **Also a mild-tasting chili, ideal for stuffing, the Anahelm has a longer, more slender shape than poblanos. (When they turn red, they're called chili colorado.) This is one of the most commonly available chilies in the United States and can be purchased fresh or canned. You can use a canned chili if that's all that's available, however, they will not hold their shape, as do fresh chilies. These chilies are commonly used as a base in salsas.**

Chipotle chilies: **Dried and smoked jalapeños, they are available dried, pickled, powdered, and canned in an adobo sauce. These chilies are dark-reddish-brown, have a distinctive chocolatey flavor, and are wonderful for use in sauces.**

Hatch chilies: **It will be rare for you to find these chilies fresh unless you're visiting New Mexico, where they are grown.**

Hatch Valley is situated in the New Mexico Chile Belt along the fertile valley of the Rio Grande. The chilies from this region are considered the best chilies in the world because of the ideal growing conditions there. Hatch peppers range from sweet bell peppers to the extra-hot Santa Fe Grande and Espanola Improved, with Big Jim's being the most ideal for stuffing. Big Jim's chilies range from mild to medium on the heat scale. Guests of the region always marvel at the big roasting drums along the streets where the smell of roasted chilies wafts through the town. To find out more about Hatch chilies, check their website at hotchile.com/hatch.htm.

Poblano chilies: **This is a large and mild chili that has a deep-blackish-green color. When cooking with poblanos, it's advisable to remove the skin and the seeds before cooking. Poblanos are ideal for stuffing and work well with cheese in such traditional Mexican dishes as chile rellenos.**

For braver tastes, you can turn to habanero, Thai, or Scotch bonnet chilies, all of which should be reserved for use in minute amounts, if at all, because they are so hot.

## *Tamales*

The possibilities for filling tamales are endless. Traditionally, tamales are filled with shredded beef, pork, or cheese and mole sauce. Because I am always striving to incorporate fresh ingredients, our tamale relies on chilies, artichoke hearts, and onion for its "meat." You won't be disappointed.

**Preparation Time: I hour ▪ Cooking Time: I hour, I5 minutes ▪ Makes 4 servings**

▪ ▪ ▪

12 corn husks

**FILLING**
1 small red onion, diced
½ cup water
⅓ cup chopped fresh or canned mild green chilies
½ cup chopped marinated artichoke hearts
⅛ teaspoon salt
⅛ teaspoon ground cumin
1 cup grated aged Gouda, Monterey Jack cheese, or queso

**CORN DOUGH**
2 cups coarsely ground masa (page 137)
1 teaspoon baking powder
1 teaspoon salt
⅔ cup grapeseed or other mild oil
⅔ cup vegetable broth

1. Place the corn husks in a large pot of water and simmer for about 45 minutes.

2. To make the filling: In a medium skillet, cook the onion and water over medium-high heat until the onion is softened.

3. Add the chilies, artichoke hearts, salt, cumin, and cheese and cook over low heat until warmed through and the cheese has melted.

4. To make the dough: In a bowl, combine the masa, baking powder, and salt. Add the oil and broth and mix to a stiff dough.

5. To assemble the tamales: Place the corn husks on a flat work surface. Lay a corn husk out flat and place 2 tablespoons of the dough in the center, spreading the batter with the back of a spoon, until it makes a 3- to 4-inch square, leaving room around the edges of the corn husk to seal it. Place a spoonful of the filling into the center and roll the tamale from one long edge to the other. Tie the open ends of the tamale with a little string or with strands of corn husks to seal it.

6. Place the tamales in a stovetop steamer. Steam for 1 hour. Serve hot.

**Note:** Tamales can be frozen for up to 2 months in a well-sealed container.

## Masa

*Masa* is the Spanish word for "dough," such as that used in tamales. It's made with sun- or fire-dried corn kernels that have been cooked then soaked in lime water overnight. The wet corn is ground into masa. The dried corn flour that looks like fine cornmeal is called *masa harina,* meaning "corn flour."

# Mediterranean Vegetable Strata

*This beautiful vegetable strata was one of the first lessons I was given in Middle Eastern cooking. I was in the American home of a woman from Iran, sipping on a glass of Assam tea, perfumed with a little Earl Grey and sweetened with crystalline lumps of rock sugar. The smells of peppers, onions, turmeric, and lemon peel wafted through the air as this rich concoction of vegetables stewed in its own juices.*

*As much as I love the version I was taught, this type of dish begs for improvisation both in the vegetables used and the addition of your favorite spices. One option is to replace the potatoes with sweet potatoes and red bell peppers for the green to create a sweeter flavor.*

**Preparation Time: 30 minutes ▪ Cooking Time: 45 minutes ▪ Makes 8 servings**

■ ■ ■

2 large onions, sliced

¼ cup extra-virgin olive oil

⅔ cup tomato paste

2 teaspoons turmeric

Salt and freshly ground black pepper, to taste

Pinch dried lemon peel

2 russet potatoes, peeled and cut into thin slices

2 green bell peppers, thinly sliced

3 carrots, peeled and thinly sliced

1 globe eggplant, peeled and cut into ½-inch-thick slices

Chopped fresh parsley

3 tablespoons fresh lemon juice

1½ cups vegetable broth

Persian Potatoes and Rice (page 185), to serve

1. In a large skillet, cook the onions in the olive oil over medium-high heat until the onions are well browned.

2. Add the tomato paste, turmeric, salt, black pepper, and lemon peel. Cook for 2 minutes.

3. In a large skillet that has a tight-fitting lid, layer the vegetables, potatoes first, then bell peppers, carrots, and eggplant. Dot the tomato paste mixture over each layer of vegetables, season with salt, and sprinkle parsley over each layer of vegetables.

4. Add pepper and lemon juice to the broth. Pour the broth over the layered vegetables.

5. Cover the skillet and cook on the stovetop over medium-high heat for 5 to 10 minutes, until the liquid begins to boil. Reduce the heat to medium-low and cook for 30 to 40 minutes, until the vegetables are soft.

6. Serve over Persian Potatoes and Rice.

# *Kuku Sabzi*

## (HERB OMELET)

*Whenever I have overindulged in the wrong kinds of foods, I crave this recipe, perhaps much as our feline and canine companions crave grass when they have upset stomachs. This is because this "omelet" recipe is comprised of handfuls of herbs. Egg is used only to bind the other ingredients together. Add savory spices and a cool, somewhat tart yogurt drizzle and you have a mouthwatering herbal classic.*

*This version of Kuku Sabzi is from the Persian mother of the owner of the Moustache Cafe in Vancouver, B.C. I've made slight amendments to accommodate my own taste and to substitute hard-to-find ingredients.*

**Preparation Time: 20 minutes ▪ Cooking Time: 10 minutes ▪ Makes 2 servings**

▪ ▪ ▪

1 bunch fresh dill

1 bunch fresh curly parsley

2 bunches fresh chives

¼ cup finely chopped walnuts (toasted, optional)

2 tablespoons finely chopped dried cranberries

1 tablespoon all-purpose flour

1 teaspoon turmeric

½ teaspoon salt

2 teaspoons fennel seeds, ground with a mortar and pestle

4 eggs, lightly beaten

Vegetable oil, for cooking

1 tablespoon butter

**YOGURT SAUCE**

⅓ cup plain yogurt

1 tablespoon plain lemon juice

1 tablespoon seasoned rice vinegar

Salt and freshly ground black pepper, to taste

1. Finely chop the dill, parsley, and chives and place them in a mixing bowl. Add the walnuts, cranberries, flour, turmeric, salt, and fennel and toss together.

2. Add the eggs and mix well.

3. Heat an omelet pan on medium-high heat. Brush the pan with oil. Pour the egg mixture into the pan and spread it evenly. Reduce the heat to medium-low and cook for 2 minutes.

4. Add the butter by rubbing it around the rim of the pan and letting it melt down the sides. Cook for 3 minutes. Flip it to the other side with a spatula and cook for 4 minutes.

5. To make the Yogurt Sauce: While the omelet is cooking, mix all the sauce ingredients together in a small bowl and set aside.

6. Drizzle the Yogurt Sauce over the finished omelet and serve hot.

# Curried Rice With Vegetables and Nuts

*When dining in a restaurant or from a street kiosk in India, you'll notice that many of the dishes are meals in a bowl. The sounds of sizzling and popping of oils and sauces in large skillets and woks waft through the streets. Fresh vegetables and meats are combined with noodles or rice to create a flavorful and fresh meal that can be consumed quickly.*

*Here, the earthiness of green curry paste, the crunch of slivered almonds, and the sweet, rich quality of coconut milk make this a particularly satisfying meal in a bowl.*

**Preparation Time: 30 minutes ▪ Cooking Time: 35 minutes ▪ Makes 6 servings**

▪ ▪ ▪

1 medium onion, chopped

1 red or yellow bell pepper, thinly sliced

2 tablespoons water

3 teaspoons curry powder (if yours is very spicy, adjust to taste)

1 teaspoon Green Curry Paste (page 144), or purchased

3 cups vegetable broth

2 cups brown basmati rice

2 cups broccoli florets

2 cups cauliflower florets

1 small carrot, peeled and cut into julienne strips

1 tablespoon minced garlic

15-ounce can coconut milk (unsweetened)

½ cup toasted slivered almonds

1. Choose a large skillet with a tight-fitting lid. Cook the onion, pepper, and water over medium-high heat for about 5 minutes until the onion is soft.

2. Add the curry powder, Green Curry Paste, and vegetable broth. Stir well.

3. Add the rice. Bring the mixture to a soft boil, then reduce the heat to low. Cover and cook for about 30 minutes, until the rice is tender.

4. While the rice is cooking, bring a large pot of water to a boil and blanch the broccoli, cauliflower, and carrot for 1 minute.

5. When the rice is finished cooking, stir in the garlic and coconut milk along with the blanched vegetables. Heat through, but do not bring to a boil again. Stir in the almonds just before serving.

## Asian Seasoning Substitutes

Asian cuisine can be intimidating at times for non-Asians, because we cannot easily find the needed ingredients. But one thing I have learned over time is that the cuisines of the world are more similar than dissimilar. No matter where you are, onions, garlic, vinegar, oil, herbs, and salt, for example, are generally used.

Asian cuisine also includes citrus flavors such as lime zest, juice, and leaves as well as lemongrass, which adds a fragrant green flavor to recipes. If you can find these ingredients fresh, buy more than you need and freeze them. They will last for months in the freezer.

If you simply can't locate these ingredients fresh, you might consider playing with other more common ingredients, though they will not offer a literal substitute. Once you understand the primary spices used in any culture, you can experiment with the recipe and customize it to your tastes. For example, lemongrass can be replaced with lemon zest or a little lemon balm, or use lime zest or Asian sweet basil for kaffir lime leaves.

You can bypass these tricky ingredients and simply go for the other flavors that drive Southeast Asian cuisine such as fresh ginger, garlic, hoisin sauce, chilies, and tamarind.

# Green Curry Paste

*This aromatic green paste is what gives some Southeast Asian dishes their flair. Because this is not an ingredient commonly found in the Western pantry, I'd like to give you a couple options: buying it or making your own. If you're feeling a little adventurous and would like to fill your home with heavenly scents, then try the following recipe. I've slightly modified the original recipe from Mai Pham's lovely book,* The Best of Thai and Vietnamese Cooking *(Prima Publishing, 1996) to avoid the use of shrimp and a couple items that are difficult to find. The flavor remains essentially intact, however.*

**Preparation Time: 10 minutes  ▪  Cooking Time: 10 minutes  ▪  Makes about 1 cup**

▪ ▪ ▪

1 teaspoon cumin seeds

1 tablespoon coriander seeds

3 white peppercorns, or 1 teaspoon ground white pepper

1 fresh medium-hot chili, quartered

6 fresh mild green chilies, chopped

4 cloves garlic, sliced

4 shallots, sliced

¼ cup chopped fresh cilantro or parsley

1 teaspoon freshly grated lime zest

2 teaspoons salt

1 tablespoon extra-virgin olive oil

1. Place a small skillet over low heat and add the cumin and coriander seeds. Shake the skillet constantly and brown the seeds for 2 to 4 minutes, until they are lightly toasted. Transfer the seeds to a small bowl. Repeat the process with the peppercorns and add them to the bowl. (Skip this step if you are using ground pepper.)

2. Place the quartered chili in the skillet and cook over medium heat until brown spots begin to appear. Remove from the skillet and set aside. In the same skillet, cook the chopped chilies, garlic, and shallots until softened. Set aside.

3. Using a spice mill or mortar and pestle, grind the cumin, coriander, and peppercorns and set aside. In the mortar, pound the roasted chili, cilantro, lime zest, and salt into a fine paste.

4. Combine the spices, chili paste, and oil together and mix until smooth. Store the paste in a tightly covered container for 2 weeks in the refrigerator or 2 to 3 months in the freezer. Freeze the paste in 2-tablespoon portions or in an ice cube tray, because that is the most you would likely use at one time.

# Red Pepper Ravioli

*I love this dish! For such a simple ravioli, the taste is exceptional. Prepackaged wonton skins are a common trick chefs use for a quick, sheer ravioli skin. The ricotta, white pepper, red bell pepper, and Parmesan give this ravioli a light and delicate taste that needs little more than a drizzle of olive oil or butter to make your taste buds sing.*

**Preparation Time: 45 minutes ▪ Cooking Time: 10 minutes ▪ Makes 16 large raviolis or 4 servings**

▪ ▪ ▪

½ cup finely chopped red bell pepper

2 tablespoons water

⅔ cup ricotta cheese

½ cup shredded Parmesan cheese or Grana Padano

Salt, to taste

White pepper

32 wonton wrappers

Water or vegetable broth, for cooking the ravioli

**TOPPING**

3 to 4 tablespoons butter (see Variation below)

4 tablespoons chopped fresh sage

1. In a medium skillet, cook the bell pepper and water over medium heat for 2 to 3 minutes, until the bell pepper has softened.

2. In a bowl, combine the ricotta, Parmesan, salt, and white pepper. Add the bell peppers and mix well.

3. On a work surface, place a wonton wrapper in front of you. Put 1 tablespoon the filling on the wonton wrapper. Moisten the edges of the wonton with water and place

another wonton wrapper on top of the first. Press around the edges with your fingers. Seal the wontons by pressing around the edges with the tines of a fork.

4. Fill a large pot with lightly salted water or vegetable broth and bring it to a gentle boil. Place the wontons in the gently boiling water and cook for 3 to 4 minutes. If the water is brought to a hard boil, the tender raviolis can break apart.

5. To make the topping: In a separate pan, melt the butter and add the sage.

6. Remove the raviolis with a slotted spoon and place them in a serving bowl. Drizzle the sage butter over the top of the raviolis and serve hot.

**Variation** Extra-virgin olive oil can be used in the place of the butter. Simply add a little salt to the oil along with the sage.

# Asparagus-Stuffed Bell Peppers

*The larger presence of year-round produce as well as vast array of frozen vegetables picked at the peak of ripeness make this dish possible on a year-round basis, as fresh asparagus is normally only seasonal. If asparagus is in season, use either the thin baby asparagus spears or white asparagus if available.*

*For vegans, substitute egg replacer for the egg, which is used as a binder.*

**Preparation Time: 30 minutes ▪ Cooking Time: I hour ▪ Makes 4 servings**

▪ ▪ ▪

4 small to medium red bell peppers

1 tablespoon vegetable oil

½ cup diced onion

½ cup peeled, ½-long asparagus pieces

Pinch nutmeg (preferably freshly grated)

½ teaspoon seasoning salt

Freshly ground black pepper

⅔ cup freshly grated Parmesan cheese

1 cup cooked white rice

1 egg, lightly beaten

½ cup vegetable broth

1. Preheat the oven to 325F (165C). Wash and slice the stem tops off the bell peppers. With your fingers, pull out the cores and seeds of the peppers.

2. Prepare a bowl of ice water and set aside. Bring a large pot of water to a boil. Place the peppers in the water and boil for 3 minutes. Remove the peppers with a slotted spoon. Place them immediately into the ice water until cool to stop the cooking, then remove and drain.

3. In a medium skillet, cook the onion in the oil over medium heat for 1 to 2 minutes, until it starts becoming tender.

4. Add the asparagus and cook until crisp-tender, about 2 minutes. Do not overcook; the asparagus should have snap left, along with some charred spots.

5. In a bowl, combine the asparagus and all the remaining ingredients.

6. Place the peppers in a baking dish and stuff each pepper with equal portions of the asparagus stuffing.

7. Bake for 1 hour, until filling is set. Serve hot.

# Roasted Beet and Pecan Risotto

*It can be a bit of a challenge at times to come up with new recipes, because it seems as if everything under the sun has already been done. But when you close your eyes, think food, and let your mind roam, all sorts of lovely things can happen. That's what I do—daydream recipes into reality. This recipe was one such whimsy. The following risotto is a marriage between Eastern Europe and Italy, as fresh, sweet beets adorn this classic risotto dish along with toasted fresh pecans. The finished product is filling, delicate, and delicious.*

*Pecorino, which is a sharp, sheep milk cheese, is used in the place of Parmesan cheese, but Parmesan will work as well.*

**Preparation Time: 30 minutes ▪ Cooking Time: I hour ▪ Makes 4 to 6 servings**

▪ ▪ ▪

> 1 small beet, peeled and cut into ½-inch cubes
> Salt and freshly ground black pepper, to taste
> Extra-virgin olive oil
> ⅔ cup pecans
> 1 medium onion, finely chopped
> 1 to 2 tablespoons butter
> 1½ cups arborio rice
> 2 cups water
> 1 teaspoon salt
> 5 ounces pecorino or Parmesan cheese, grated finely

1. Preheat the oven to 350F (180C). Place the beet in a baking dish. Sprinkle it with salt and pepper and drizzle with olive oil. Bake for 20 to 25 minutes, until the beet is softened, but still has a little resistance when cut with a butter knife.

2. Meanwhile, chop the pecans and place them on a small baking sheet. Toast in the oven alongside the beet for 6 to 8 minutes, until they are lightly browned.

3. Place the onion and the butter in a large skillet that can be covered. Cook over medium heat for 3 to 5 minutes, until the onion is browned.

4. Add the rice, 2 cups water, and 1 teaspoon salt. Bring to a boil, and reduce the heat to low. Simmer the rice until the water is almost gone, stirring frequently. Have a pot of boiling water with a ladle on the next burner. Add small amounts of water, as needed, until the rice reaches the desired consistency. This can take 20 to 30 minutes. As with all risotto dishes, the consistency of the rice is a matter of personal preference.

5. When the risotto is finished cooking, remove from the stove and add the grated cheese. Stir well.

6 Transfer the risotto to a serving bowl. Spoon the beet and pecans over the top and serve hot.

# *Vegetable Bread Pudding*

The richness imparted by such dishes as this scrumptious vegetable bread pudding is the hallmark of Cajun cuisine. This means you need to find a good balance between fats from dairy and fresh produce to create a healthful meal.

This dish was inspired by a similarly titled dish I was served as an entrée at a chic Market Street restaurant in San Francisco. There was so much cream, however, that it was purely sinful. So I've lightened it up a bit to relieve us of the angst and guilt. To lighten it up further, you can substitute the half-and-half with fat-free (skim) evaporated milk.

**Preparation Time: 40 minutes ▪ Cooking Time: 50 minutes ▪ Makes 6 servings**

▪ ▪ ▪

2 cups thinly sliced asparagus

1 cup sliced mushrooms

2 cups sliced yellow crookneck squash

½ teaspoon seasoning salt

2 tablespoons minced garlic

3 tablespoons water

3 cups cubed sweet French bread, crusts cut off

Salt, to taste

½ teaspoon herbes de Provence

¾ cup chopped fresh chives

1 cup grated Gouda cheese

1 cup grated fontina cheese

½ cup freshly grated Parmesan cheese

5 eggs

2½ cups half–and–half, fat-free evaporated milk, or soy cream

White pepper

½ teaspoon freshly grated nutmeg

1. Preheat the oven to 400F (205C). Lightly butter a soufflé dish. In a medium skillet, cook the asparagus, mushrooms, squash, seasoning salt, garlic, and water over medium-high heat until the vegetables have softened.

2. In a large bowl, mix the bread cubes, salt, herbes de Provence, and chives.

3. Combine the Gouda, fontina, and Parmesan cheeses in a small bowl; reserve ½ cup for the topping. Toss the vegetables and remaining cheeses with the bread mixture. Place the mixture into prepared soufflé dish.

4. In a bowl, lightly beat the eggs. Add the half-and-half, salt, white pepper, and nutmeg. Mix well, then pour the egg mixture over the bread mixture. Sprinkle the reserved ½ cup cheese over the top.

5. Bake for 40 minutes, or until set. Serve directly from the oven.

## Seasoning Salt

The term *seasoning salt* encompasses a broad array of ingredients combined with salt to create a product that enables the cook to easily add some complexity to the flavor of a dish.

Some of the better-quality seasoning salts will contain finely ground herbs as well as an array of spices that complement many savory dishes. Others are less complex in their flavors, but can still be useful to have in the pantry.

One thing to be aware of when purchasing a seasoning salt is that some contain monosodium glutamate (MSG) as a general flavor enhancer. I am not a proponent of the use of MSG in the diet, and I would recommend using a natural seasoning salt that has been created with a quality blend of spices and herbs that suits your palate.

# *Green Gumbo*

*It's hard to imagine a gumbo without that rich, smoky taste derived from cured meats. To keep it light, we've replaced the meat with hickory-smoked tofu and olive oil with a surprisingly good result. And you will note that none of the flavor is missing from this healthful dish.*

**Preparation Time: 30 minutes** ▪ **Cooking Time: 30 minutes** ▪ **Makes 4 servings**
▪ ▪ ▪

½ cup plus 2 tablespoons extra-virgin olive oil

⅔ cup all-purpose flour

2 cups chopped onions

1 red bell pepper, chopped

2 shallots, minced

1 cup quartered carrot slices

4 teaspoons Cajun seasoning

2 tablespoons minced garlic

4 cups vegetable broth

2 cups water

6 ounces hickory-baked tofu, crumbled

1 bunch collard greens, cleaned, stemmed, and chopped

½ bunch chard, cleaned, stemmed, and chopped

½ bunch kale, cleaned, stemmed, and chopped

4 cups cooked rice (optional)

Salt, to taste

1. Make a roux (page 156) by whisking together the ½ cup olive oil and flour in a small skillet. Cook over medium heat, stirring constantly, until the roux just begins to brown. Remove the roux from the heat immediately or it will burn. Set aside to cool.

2. In a large pot, cook the onions and bell pepper in the 2 tablespoons olive oil over medium heat until soft. Add the shallots and cook for 1 minute.

3. Add the carrots, Cajun seasoning, garlic, broth, and water. Bring to a boil, stir in the roux, and cook for 10 to 15 minutes, until the carrots are cooked and the soup just comes to a boil. If the soup is too thick, add a little more broth or water.

4. Add the tofu and greens and remove from the heat. The rice can be added at this time (if used). Season with salt. Serve hot.

## Filé Powder and Cajun Spices

The most many of us know about filé powder is from Hank Williams's song, "Jambalaya." Remember? "Jambalaya/ crawfish pie/filé gumbo . . ." In fact, I'm listening to it now via the Internet! Now that things are jumping around he-ha, I'm ready to tell you more about this indispensable spice of the bayou.

In short, filé powder is dried wild sassafras leaves that have been ground into a powder. It was the Choctaw Indians from the Louisiana bayous who are thought to have been the first users of filé powder. Since then, it has become an integral part of Creole cooking, used at the base of gumbos and soups and added at the last minute as flavoring and as a thickening agent in filé gumbo. The reason it's added after the heat is turned off is because it becomes tough and stringy when overheated.

Cajun spice seasoning is relatively easy to find in supermarkets today. Each blend carries its own distinct flavor, and it's really up to the taste of the cook as to which is better. In general, Cajun spice blends include the following ingredients, just in case you would like to try making your own: garlic powder, onion powder, ground chilies, black pepper, dry mustard, and ground celery seed. Bold and pungent would be an apt description of this seasoning blend.

# Dirty Rice and Beans

*I never have cared much for the name of this dish, but anyone who has enjoyed a traditional dinner in Louisiana knows that dirty rice and beans is not an option, but mandatory—as it should be! Onions, garlic, and Cajun seasoning give this rice dish a kick that you'll remember.*

*To replace the meat traditionally used in this dish, we are using smoked seitan, which is also referred to as "wheat meat." It has a surprisingly similar flavor and texture to beef but is made of wheat gluten.*

**Preparation Time: 15 minutes** ▪ **Cooking Time: 30 minutes** ▪ **Makes 6 servings**

▪ ▪ ▪

1½ cups chopped onions

1 red bell pepper, chopped

2 tablespoons olive oil

2 cups white basmati rice

1 teaspoon minced garlic

1 tablespoon Cajun seasoning

3 cups vegetable broth

1 cup cubed barbecued or smoked seitan

1 cup cooked red kidney beans

1 cup chopped fresh or canned tomatoes

Salt and freshly ground black pepper, to taste

## Roux

Roux is the classic thickening agent used at the base of Southern Louisiana soups and gumbos as well as sauces. Roux is simply equal portions of some sort of oil or fat and flour cooked until it reaches a beige or brown color. For the deep-brown roux popular in much of Creole cooking, butter or bacon fat is used. For the purposes of a vegetarian cookbook, we use butter. Other, lighter oils can also be used to create a lighter-colored roux that can be used at the base of creamy-colored sauces. For those who do not wish to use animal products such as butter, oil is a good alternative. Once it's incorporated into a lively Creole dish, it's unlikely anyone will be able to distinguish a butter-based roux from oil.

Do keep in mind that the darker you choose to brown the flour, the more the starch compound breaks down, making it less effective as a thickening agent, and increasing the possibility of burning.

1. In a large skillet with a cover, cook the onions and red bell pepper in the olive oil over medium heat until the onions are caramelized.

2. Add the rice, garlic, Cajun seasoning, and broth. Bring to a simmer.

3. Add the seitan, cover, and cook for about 30 minutes, until the rice is tender.

4. Add the kidney beans and tomatoes, and cook just long enough to warm them through. Season with salt and pepper and serve hot.

# Potato-Chive Soufflé

*One issue I've had with potato soufflés in the past is that they sometimes tend to be on the bland side. In order to avoid your having the same experience, we've added nutmeg, chives, white pepper, and Parmesan cheese to bring a very elegant blend of flavors to this light and fluffy potato dish.*

**Preparation Time: 30 minutes ▪ Cooking Time: 45 minutes ▪ Makes 4 to 6 servings**

▪ ▪ ▪

2½ tablespoons butter

3 tablespoons all-purpose flour

1 cup milk, heated until hot

Pinch nutmeg (preferably freshly grated)

Salt and white pepper, to taste

4 egg yolks

1½ cups mashed potatoes

1 bunch fresh chives, finely chopped

1 tablespoon minced fresh parsley

5 egg whites

½ cup freshly grated Parmesan cheese

1. Butter a 1-quart soufflé dish. Place an oven rack in the lower third of the oven and preheat the oven to 400F (205C).

2. In a medium saucepan, melt the butter over medium heat. Stir in the flour and cook, stirring frequently, for 3 minutes. Do not let it brown. Remove the saucepan from the heat and let it cool for 1 minute, then add the hot milk and whisk until blended. Return the saucepan to the heat, bring to a slow boil, and boil for 3 minutes. Whisk in the nutmeg, salt, and pepper and remove from the heat.

3. Whisk in the egg yolks one at a time, mixing well after each yolk is added. Next, mix in the mashed potatoes, chives, and parsley.

4. In a separate bowl, beat the egg whites with an electric mixer on high speed until stiff peaks form.

5. Add a little egg white (about ½ cup) to the potato mixture and stir well. Then fold in the remaining egg whites quickly and lightly, sprinkling in the Parmesan cheese as you fold. Spoon the mixture into the soufflé dish and place in the oven. Reduce the heat to 375F (190C). Bake for 20 to 25 minutes, until the soufflé has puffed and the top has browned nicely. Serve immediately.

## Soufflé Tips

Light as a cloud and delicate on the tongue, you would think soufflés would be a standard part of any cook's repertoire. Unfortunately, the word brings more cringes than coos. Understandably. If you've ever experienced the disaster of a flattened soufflé, you're unlikely to try again anytime soon. Let's see if we can take some of the chance out of the soufflé game. The key is in scrupulous preparation. The creamy base, be it a sauce or puree (this is the part that carries the flavor), must be resting at room temperature. So must the egg whites. The baking dish should be buttered and chilled.

The basics taken care of, the rest depends on beating the egg whites until they form stiff, glossy peaks, using a gentle hand in folding in the puree or sauce, and knowing when to remove the soufflé from the oven.

When beating the egg whites, it's important to start with clean beaters and bowl; a copper bowl is best. If you do not have a copper bowl, add just a pinch of cream of tartar to the egg whites before beating.

Once the puree is folded into the egg whites and the mixture has been turned into the buttered dish, place the soufflé in the bottom third of the oven, otherwise you may end up with a leathery crust. Close the oven door gently and wait. This is where trust comes in to play. You can't peek, as you'll alter the oven temperature by opening the door or risk a collapse in closing the door too hard.

Good luck!

# Avocado and Baby Greens Tacos

*Many people still think of Southwestern cuisine as a rack of baby-back ribs slathered with barbecue sauce. Not true. Some of the nation's and world's best chefs have chosen to spend their days in perpetual sunshine and have brought all their talents to places like Tucson, Phoenix, Sedona, and Santa Fe. For this reason you'll find much lighter and fresher Southwestern fare than what was available in the past. This recipe uses both the sharp taste of Parmesan and the milder Mexican cheese called panela to give a fresh and lively lift to these bright little avocado tacos.*

**Preparation Time: 30 minutes • Cooking Time: 5 minutes • Makes 12 tacos**

■ ■ ■

12 corn tortillas
Vegetable oil for cooking
½ cup very finely grated Parmesan cheese
2 avocados, sliced
2 tomatoes, chopped
1 onion, chopped
1 cup grated panela, ricotta salata, or Cheddar cheese
8 ounces assorted baby greens
1 cup salsa

1. Heat a medium skillet over medium-high heat. Brush the heated skillet with a little oil, add a tortilla, and cook for about 30 seconds,

## About Mexican Cheese

It wasn't until a few years ago that I began exploring the world of Mexican cheeses, and what a surprise I found. While some of the cheeses are extremely mild and soft, others are drier and have a more pronounced flavor. One of my favorites is called panela. If you cannot find this cheese, another very similar one is called ricotta salata, which is a dry ricotta cheese. Ricotta salata is not a Mexican cheese, but it has similar properties and could complement tacos.

For a soft-potted cheese, try the queso blanco, which is also called queso fresco. This can be used in the place of fresh ricotta and is similar to farmer cheese. It's found in cottage cheese–style tubs in Latin markets and supermarkets.

Another cheese to look for is queso anejo. Made from cow milk, as are all the others, this white cheese is made from skim milk, and has a much stronger flavor than queso blanco or panela.

until hot. Remove the tortilla and quickly sprinkle the cooked side with very finely grated Parmesan cheese. Repeat with remaining tortillas and Parmesan cheese.

2. Layer the avocados, tomatoes, onion, panela, and greens over the Parmesan cheese on each tortilla. Top with salsa. Serve immediately.

# *Quinoa-Stuffed Zucchini*

*I spoke of the wonders of quinoa in Quinoa and Wild Rice Salad (page 56). In this recipe, we have incorporated it to make a wonderful-tasting and highly nutritious stuffed zucchini. Fresh herbs, sun-dried tomatoes, and a generous amount of Asiago cheese make this zucchini dish shine!*

**Preparation Time: 30 minutes ▪ Cooking Time: 45 minutes ▪ Makes 4 servings**

▪ ▪ ▪

4 medium zucchini

1 cup vegetable broth

Pinch salt

1/2 cup quinoa

1/3 cup finely chopped sun-dried tomatoes (oil-packed or dried)

2 Roma tomatoes, chopped

1 tablespoon chopped fresh herbs, such as parsley, oregano, tarragon, and rosemary

1/2 cup bread crumbs

1/4 teaspoon salt

1/8 teaspoon freshly ground black pepper

1 egg, lightly beaten

1/2 cup finely grated hard cheese, such as Asiago, Parmesan, aged Gouda, or Old Amsterdam

1 to 2 tablespoons butter, melted

1. In a large pot of water, boil the zucchini whole for 8 minutes. Remove the zucchini from the water and allow to cool.

2. Preheat the oven to 375F (190C). In a small saucepan, bring the broth and pinch salt to a boil. Add the quinoa and sun-dried tomatoes. Bring back to a boil and reduce the heat to low. Cover and simmer for 15 minutes.

3. Cut the ends off of the cooled zucchini. Slice the zucchinis lengthwise and scoop out the pulp with a teaspoon.

4. Chop the zucchini pulp and place it into a mixing bowl. Add the Roma tomatoes, herbs, half the bread crumbs, 1/4 teaspoon salt, pepper, egg, cheese, and quinoa mixture. Mix well.

5. Spoon the mixture into the cavity of the zucchini halves. Sprinkle remaining bread crumbs on top of the filling and drizzle the butter lightly over the top.

6. Place the stuffed zucchini halves on a baking sheet. Bake for 15 to 20 minutes, until the stuffing is firm. Serve hot.

## Quinoa

The ancient Incas called quinoa (pronounced keen-wa) "the mother grain." Once you understand the nutritional significance of this grainlike seed, you can see why it enjoyed an elevated status. Not only is quinoa higher in protein than grains, it also qualifies as a complete protein. This means it contains all eight essential amino acids (the components of protein). Quinoa is also lower in carbohydrates than most grains, higher in fat, and contains a rich array of vitamins and minerals. Another benefit of adding quinoa to the diet is that it is easy to digest.

Quinoa's tiny, bead-shape size lends itself to quick cooking, taking about half the time it takes to cook rice. It plumps up to four times its size and can be used in the place of rice or couscous in a wide variety of recipes. Another use for quinoa is as a super nutrient-rich hot breakfast cereal. Cultivated in South America for thousands of years, quinoa is now being grown domestically as well and can be found in most natural food stores.

# On the Side, Please

■ ■ ■

Anything goes here. Although side dishes are generally an accompaniment to the main course, there is nothing stopping a dish relegated to the "side dish" category from stepping up to the plate as the star feature.

As with appetizers, I often prefer to make a meal of side dishes whether dining in or out. In fact, I've been known to embarrass many a dining companion while attempting to recreate the menu to my liking at some unsuspecting little bistro. I generally use the excuse that I'm a vegetarian and there is not a full meal on the menu oriented toward nonmeat eaters. Waiters and chefs with good dispositions will often accommodate me as I order the garlic potatoes off the prime rib menu, the teriyaki green beans from the glazed chicken menu, and the pine nut and currant cole slaw that generally accompanies the fresh catch of the day to create my own entrée plate. (I must say here that these requests are more often than not met with sour glances and more than a little resistance, so I am not suggesting that you subject your server to this kind of challenge.)

The point of this discourse is to suggest that you may choose to break out of the box with your side dishes, as there are many recipes in this chapter that could as easily take center stage. Besides, nobody's going to give you a hard time if you play mix 'n' match in your own kitchen.

# Caribbean Cooked Rice

*There is a sweetness that permeates all of life in the Caribbean, including its cuisine. The following rice recipe has a distinctly aromatic, spicy, and sweet flavor and can be served alongside Caribbean Vegetable Stew (page 68). It also stands on its own served with a fresh fruit–based salad such as the Avocado-Pineapple Salad with Honey-Lime Dressing (page 41).*

**Preparation Time: 15 minutes ▪ Cooking Time: 30 to 40 minutes ▪ Makes 4 to 6 servings**

▪ ▪ ▪

> 2 cups water
> 1 cup milk
> 1/3 cup canned or fresh coconut milk (unsweetened)
> 1 cup white rice
> 1/2 teaspoon salt
> Pinch nutmeg
> Pinch cinnamon
> Grated zest of 1 orange
> 1/2 cup fresh or dried unsweetened shredded coconut
> 1/4 cup sugar
> 1/4 cup raisins
> 1 teaspoon pure vanilla extract
> 1/4 teaspoon pure almond extract

1. Heat the water, milk, and coconut milk in a large saucepan over medium-high heat until boiling. Add the rice, salt, nutmeg, cinnamon, and orange zest. Cook, stirring frequently as with a risotto, for about 20 minutes until the rice is partially done.

2. Add the coconut, sugar, raisins, vanilla extract, and almond extract. Cook until the rice reaches the desired texture, adding water when necessary. Serve hot.

# Mashed Sweet Potatoes
## with Cloves and Molasses

*Yum! Like in sweet potato pie, molasses and cloves bring the soul to this simple yet scrumptious side dish. In addition to the comfort they bring to this dish, sweet potatoes have been found to have one of the highest concentrations of vitamin A as well as vitamin C in the vegetable kingdom. As a vegetable superstar, sweet potatoes are also rich in fiber and complex carbohydrates, so enjoy!*

**Preparation Time: 20 minutes ▪ Cooking Time: 30 minutes ▪ Makes 3 cups; 3 to 4 servings**

▪ ▪ ▪

> **4 Garnet sweet potatoes**
> **½ teaspoon salt**
> **⅛ teaspoon ground cloves**
> **2 tablespoons unsalted butter**
> **2 tablespoons molasses**

1. Preheat the oven to 350F (180C). Scrub the sweet potatoes and wrap them in foil. Bake 45 to 60 minutes, depending on the size of the sweet potatoes, until soft.

2. When the sweet potatoes are cool enough to handle, slit open the top and scoop out the flesh.

3. Mash or puree the flesh in a food processor until smooth.

4. Add the remaining ingredients to the food processor and mix well. Transfer to a serving bowl. Serve warm.

# Pea Shoots in Chinese Five-Spice Sauce

*This recipe is about green. You can taste and feel the freshness of "green" from the tender baby pea shoots. Pea shoots (from garden peas, not sweet pea flowers) are historically grown seasonally, but with the advent of hothouse agriculture, you can find them year-round now in many Asian food stores. For a light, healthful meal, serve with the Green Onion Pancakes (page 3).*

**Preparation Time: 10 minutes ▪ Cooking Time: 5 minutes ▪ Makes 4 servings**

▪ ▪ ▪

2 tablespoons water
1 pound fresh pea shoots
1 teaspoon minced garlic
1 teaspoon Chinese five-spice powder
1 teaspoon sesame oil

1. Heat a skillet over medium-high heat and add the water, pea shoots, garlic, and five-spice powder. Cook, tossing together, for about 3 minutes, until just wilted.

2. Stir in the sesame oil. Serve hot.

# Sautéed Tofu in Mushroom Sauce

*The chief complaint of cooks unfamiliar with tofu is that it is bland. I prefer the word* neutral. *The beauty of tofu is that it takes on the flavors of any ingredient it's paired with, so there is no limit to the intensity and variety of flavors one can create with tofu as the chief ingredient. Here, fresh ginger, green onions, shallots, and rice vinegar add the sizzle to this highly flavorful tofu dish served with a mixed mushroom sauce.*

**Preparation Time: 30 minutes • Cooking Time: 15 minutes • Makes 4 servings**

1 tablespoon minced shallot

2 tablespoons water or vegetable broth

1 tablespoon grated fresh ginger

1 cup vegetable or mushroom broth

½ cup soy sauce

2 tablespoons plain rice vinegar

4 ounces fresh shitake mushrooms, sliced

4 ounces button mushrooms, sliced, or substitute oyster, portabello, or crimini mushrooms

½ cup dried Chinese black mushrooms, reconstituted in boiling water

4 pounds snow peas

1 pound firm tofu, cubed

1 bunch green onions (green and white parts), trimmed and chopped

1. In a skillet, cook the shallot and water over medium heat, stirring, for about 5 minutes, until softened. Add the ginger, broth, soy sauce, and vinegar and stir. Add the button and Chinese black mushrooms and cook, stirring, for 5 to 8 minutes, until tender.

2. Add the peas and tofu and cook, stirring, until just heated through. Add the green onions and serve.

## Using Dry Soybeans

Like most other beans, cooking soybeans can be mildly challenging at times. The frustration can come from beans that do not cook all the way through no matter how long you've cooked them. This is often due to storage problems such as being stored at the wrong temperature or humidity level for long periods of time. However, there are quick and easy solutions to the problem.

The best option is to presoak the beans. For a faster presoaking period, boil the beans in a large amount of water for about 2 minutes, then put them in a bowl of lightly salted water to soak for an hour or two. This eliminates the need to soak overnight. Once the soaking is finished, rinse the beans and cook as the recipe calls for.

## Warning: Fresh Soybeans

You may have noticed that I did not include a recipe for edamame, fresh soybeans that have been lightly boiled, in their pods, in salted water.

The reason for this omission is somewhat personal. Although I have always loved the flavor of fresh soybeans while dining at Japanese restaurants, I noticed that I always felt bad after leaving the restaurant. My digestive process was severely upset, and it would be as much as 24 hours before I would feel up to par again. Then I came across some information about raw soybeans in Shirley Corriher's *CookWise: The Hows and Whys*

*of Successful Cooking* (William Morrow and Co., 1997). She states that raw soybeans and certain other legumes contain an enzyme inhibitor that does not allow for the digestion of proteins. Raw soybeans create chemical changes in the linings of the intestines that prohibit the absorption of nutrients. Once the soybeans are cooked, these protease inhibitors are neutralized and the beans are both safe and highly nutritious.

I can't help but think there are many others among us that are having the same reaction but might not know what to attribute it to.

# Potato Pancakes with Chives

*As a young woman working in the world of television in New York City, I was in need of just about every kind of comfort I could find. One of my fondest memories was going to my favorite Jewish delicatessen, which has since burned down, for a crispy, hot plate of potato pancakes served with sour cream and applesauce. As my love affair with potato pancakes continues, I've added chives for a little extra flavor in my version of the Eastern European favorite.*

**Preparation Time: 20 minutes (plus cooling time)** ▪ **Cooking Time: 15 minutes** ▪
**Makes 6 servings**

▪ ▪ ▪

> 3 russet potatoes, peeled
> ½ cup finely chopped chives, plus 3 tablespoons for garnish (optional)
> Salt and freshly ground black pepper, to taste
> Grapeseed oil or butter, for cooking

1. Place the whole potatoes in a steamer and steam for 12 to 15 minutes, until just tender but not floury. They must be cooked through but not overcooked or they will not hold together.

2. Cool the potatoes completely, then grate. Mix the potatoes and chives and season with salt and pepper.

3. Heat a nonstick skillet over medium-high heat. Add enough oil to coat the bottom of the skillet. Scoop about ½ cup potato mixture into your hands and form into a patty. Place the patties in the hot skillet and cook until they are browned on both sides, turning once. Garnish with chives (if using) and serve hot.

**Note:** Potatoes need to be completely cool when grated, so they could be cooked the morning of or the day before final preparation and refrigerated.

# Toasted Buckwheat

Toasted buckwheat has become a favorite of mine for breakfast. Pair it with a small bowl of yogurt and honey and a cup of green tea, or Argentine yerba mate tea, and you have a solid start to the day that boosts the immune system, stabilizes blood sugar, and keeps you going until the lunch hour.

In Eastern Europe, this nut-flavored grain is traditionally served very simply with butter and salt or can be used as a bed for vegetables such as the Root Vegetables with Sherry (page 103).

**Preparation Time: 5 minutes** ▪ **Cooking Time: 5 minutes** ▪ **Makes 2 servings**

▪ ▪ ▪

2½ cups water
1 cup kasha (toasted buckwheat)
½ teaspoon salt

1. In a saucepan, bring the water to a boil. Add the kasha and salt. Cover and cook on medium heat for about 5 minutes, stirring occasionally, until the kasha is tender.

2. Serve hot.

## Buckwheat: The Super Seed

Buckwheat is commonly thought of as a cereal grain, but it's actually a fruit seed. It comes from a plant that resembles a bush rather than a grass. It has an odd triangular shape housed in an inedible black outer shell that must be removed. The tan interior kernel is used for cereal, flour, and animal feed. Toasted buckwheat is known as kasha and is a standard part of the Eastern European diet. When you consider its dietary benefits, you may want to incorporate buckwheat into your diet as well.

Buckwheat is fairly high in protein, with, gram per gram, about half of what you would find in beef. The amino acid content compares with that of nonfat milk solids and whole eggs. Perhaps the greatest dietary benefit of buckwheat, however, is that it contains a substantial amount of the essential amino acid lysine—the highest concentration of lysine found in any cereal grain. This is an important factor because it can be challenging for a vegetarian to obtain all the essential amino acids.

Buckwheat flour is low in gluten, which means you will need to mix it with wheat flour for bread-making. I most enjoy eating toasted buckwheat for breakfast as a hot cereal. It takes only minutes to cook and has a wonderful nutty flavor from the toasting. You can pour a little milk of your choice and a light drizzle of maple syrup for a great-tasting start to the day.

# Herbed Brown and Wild Rice

*Many evenings I'm content to have a meal of herbed rice and vegetables. The chewy quality of the wild rice, mixed with the flavors of sage and the traditional French herb combination herbes de Provence, makes this simple rice dish very aromatic and satisfying as an accompaniment or a meal itself.*

**Preparation Time: 10 minutes ▪ Cooking Time: 30 minutes ▪ Makes 4 servings**

▪ ▪ ▪

3 cups vegetable broth or water

½ teaspoon garlic powder

1 teaspoon onion powder

¼ to ½ teaspoons herbes de Provence, or to taste

¼ to ½ teaspoon rubbed sage, or to taste

¼ teaspoon seasoning salt

¼ teaspoon salt

2 tablespoons olive oil or butter

¾ cup long-grain brown rice

¼ cup wild rice

1. In a saucepan, bring the broth to a boil and add all the remaining ingredients. Cover, reduce the heat to the lowest setting, and cook for about 25 minutes, or until the rice reaches the desired texture. Add a small amount of water if the rice is drying out before it is completely cooked.

2. Serve hot.

# Provençal Potato Gratin

*Because you cannot have a French menu without a dish featuring the* pomme de terre *(potato: apple of the earth), we have included a potato dish to remember! To move away from the cream-laden traditional au gratin dishes, we have used olive oil, fresh herbs, cured olives, and French feta to take potatoes au gratin to a new high on the flavor scale.*

**Preparation Time: 30 minutes ▪ Cooking Time: 30 minutes ▪ Makes 4 to 6 servings**

▪ ▪ ▪

2 pounds red or yellow Finn potatoes, cut into ¼-inch slices

1 fennel bulb, sliced

1 cup thinly sliced onion

6 Roma tomatoes, halved lengthwise

½ cup oil-cured ripe olives

⅓ cup extra-virgin olive oil

1 teaspoon herbes de Provence

1 tablespoon minced garlic

Salt and freshly ground black pepper, to taste

¼ cup freshly grated Parmesan cheese

½ cup crumbled feta cheese, preferably French feta

1. Cook the potatoes in boiling water until tender but still firm. Cook the fennel in boiling water until tender.

2. Preheat the oven to 400F (205C). In a bowl, toss the potatoes, fennel, onion, tomatoes, olives, olive oil, herbes de Provence, garlic, salt, and pepper. Transfer the potato mixture to a shallow baking dish. Sprinkle the Parmesan and feta cheeses on top of the vegetables. Bake for 20 to 30 minutes, until the onion is tender. Serve hot.

# Eggs with Chard

*This is a wonderful little meal if you're in a hurry but need a quick protein pick-up. Swiss chard is wonderful when paired with garlic and eggs or egg substitutes. A pinch of sea salt and violà!*

**Preparation Time: 15 minutes • Cooking Time: 10 minutes • Makes 1 serving**

**Butter or olive oil, for cooking**
**1 small clove garlic, finely chopped or pressed**
**3 Swiss chard leaves, torn into pieces, stems removed**
**Herbes de Provence, to taste**
**2 eggs, beaten, or ½ cup egg substitute**
**Sea salt, to taste**

1. Heat a medium skillet over medium heat. Brush the bottom with butter.

2. Add the garlic, chard, and herbes de Provence. Cook for 1 minute, until the chard is wilted.

3. In a separate bowl, combine the eggs and salt. Pour over the chard in the skillet; turn the mixture with a spatula until thoroughly cooked. Serve hot.

# *Dahl*

*Dahl is a traditional meal opener in India and can come in as many versions as the chefs who prepare it. Some dahls are very thin and light in flavor and range in appearance from brown to yellow to red, depending on the type of lentil selected. Our version is on the heartier side, and it's your choice as to the type of lentil you use. I find that red lentils make a particularly lovely dahl. They can be found in Middle Eastern and East Indian specialty shops or in health food stores along with yellow lentils, while the common brown variety are easily found in supermarkets.*

**Preparation Time: 20 minutes ▪ Cooking Time: 30 minutes ▪ Makes 4 servings**

▪ ▪ ▪

> ¾ cup dried lentils
>
> 5 to 6 cups water or vegetable broth
>
> 14.5-ounce can chopped tomatoes
>
> 1 medium onion, finely chopped
>
> 3 cloves garlic, pressed
>
> 2 tablespoons extra-virgin olive oil
>
> 1 teaspoon Garam Marsala (page 120), or purchased
>
> ½ teaspoon turmeric
>
> ½ teaspoon ground cumin
>
> Dash cayenne pepper
>
> Salt, to taste

1. Combine all the ingredients in a large saucepan. Bring to a boil over medium heat. Reduce the heat and simmer for 50 to 60 minutes, stirring occasionally, until lentils are tender. Add small amounts of water during the cooking if the mixture is becoming too thick.

2. Taste for seasoning. Serve hot.

# Curried Creamed Spinach

*One of the real joys of reaching the age of independence was scouting out the cuisines of the world. While this admittedly took place over a prolonged period of time, I have no words for the pleasure of discovering the flavors of some of the most humble dishes, like this spicy spinach side dish. East Indian spices such as garam masala and turmeric take this pureed spinach dish to new heights of pleasure.*

*As a note, when dining in an Indian restaurant, this dish would be found under the name saag paneer. The authentic dish uses a different, more astringent type of leaf, which is not easily found in Western supermarkets. This is why I have Westernized the dish with spinach and changed the name.*

**Preparation Time: 30 minutes ▪ Cooking Time: 30 minutes ▪ Makes 4 servings**

▪ ▪ ▪

1 medium onion, diced

2 to 3 Roma tomatoes, diced

2 cloves garlic, minced

2 tablespoons extra-virgin olive oil

½ teaspoon Garam Masala (page 120), or purchased

¼ teaspoon turmeric

Pinch cayenne pepper

Water, as needed

2 bunches spinach, washed and stemmed

Salt, to taste

1 cup fresh buffalo mozzarella or paneer cheese cubes

1. Place the onion, tomatoes, garlic, and oil in a large skillet and cook over medium heat for 3 to 4 minutes.

2. Add the Garam Masala, turmeric, and cayenne and simmer, adding small amounts of water as the mixture becomes dry, until the vegetables are very soft.

3. Add the spinach and simmer for 25 to 30 minutes, adding water when dry.

4. Place the mixture in a blender with just enough water to allow the mixture to move freely in the blender; puree until smooth. Season with salt.

5. Transfer the mixture from the blender to a saucepan. Reheat it over medium heat. Drop the cubes of cheese into the spinach. Serve when cheese begins to melt.

# *Risotto Milanese*

*My love for the classic Italian risotto began when a golden plate of risotto passed by my table at a small, bustling Tuscan restaurant in Milan. I noticed that all the locals seemed to be ordering the risotto for the table's first course, so I followed suit and asked the waiter to explain what was in the dish. It turned out to be a classic risotto dish with the addition of saffron. The following is my interpretation of the popular Milanese dish. I think you'll be pleased with its satisfying and delicate flavor.*

**Preparation Time: 15 minutes ▪ Cooking Time: 25 to 40 minutes ▪ Makes 6 servings**

■ ■ ■

> ½ **cup white wine**
> ⅛ **to** ¼ **teaspoon saffron threads**
> ¼ **cup very finely chopped onion**
> 1¼ **cups arborio rice**
> 2 **cups vegetable broth**
> **Salt, to taste**
> **Water, as needed**
> ¾ **to 1 cup coarsely grated Parmesan cheese**

1. In a medium saucepan, cook the wine, saffron threads, and onion over medium heat for 3 to 4 minutes.

2. Place the rice in a strainer and rinse in cold water. Add the rice, vegetable broth, and salt to the wine mixture.

3. Cook over medium-low heat, stirring frequently, adding small amounts of water when necessary, until the risotto reaches your preferred consistency. This risotto takes from 25 to 40 minutes to cook.

4. Stir in the Parmesan cheese when the risotto is finished cooking. Serve hot.

# Pasta and Fava Bean Salad

*The broad-shaped fava bean adds a creamy and nutritious dimension to this hearty pasta salad. Its fresh taste comes from the fresh Italian herbs, fresh garlic, and lemon juice.*

**Preparation Time: 30 minutes • Cooking Time: 15 minutes • Makes 4 to 6 servings**

8 ounces pennette pasta shells

1 (19-ounce) can fava beans, drained, or 2 cups cooked butter beans

1 red or yellow bell pepper, diced

1 cup chopped fresh chives (1 bunch)

¼ cup chopped fresh parsley

2 tablespoons chopped fresh basil

⅓ cup extra-virgin olive oil or flavored olive oil, such as garlic-flavored

2 to 3 cloves garlic, finely minced or pressed

2 tablespoons fresh lemon juice

¼ cup balsamic vinegar

Salt and freshly ground black pepper, to taste

1. Cook the pasta in lightly salted water according to package directions. Rinse the pasta with cold water and place it into a large mixing bowl.

2. Add all the remaining ingredients, adjusting seasonings to taste. Serve at room temperature.

# *Spanish Rice*

*I have enjoyed this Spanish rice recipe since I was a small child, as this was Mom's favorite rice dish. I would sniff the pan and hope she had made enough for leftovers, because, somehow, the dish seemed to taste even better the next day. In all its simplicity, I have not been able to top this family favorite.*

**Preparation Time: 20 minutes ▪ Cooking Time: 30 minutes ▪ Makes 6 servings**

▪ ▪ ▪

    1 onion, chopped

    2/3 green bell pepper, chopped

    2 tablespoons extra-virgin olive oil

    2¾ cups water

    1 cup white basmati rice

    1½ tablespoons spicy yellow or brown mustard

    2/3 cup tomato sauce

    2¼ cups water

    Salt and freshly ground black pepper, to taste

1. In a large skillet that can be tightly covered, cook the onion, bell pepper, olive oil, and ½ cup water over medium heat until the vegetables are tender.

2. Stir in the rice, mustard, tomato sauce, remaining 2½ cups water, salt, and pepper. Bring to a boil over medium-high heat, stirring frequently. Reduce the heat to low, cover, and simmer for 20 to 25 minutes. Check the rice after 15 minutes to see if more water is needed. Serve hot.

# Lentils with Spinach and Feta

*One of the primary sources of protein in the Middle Eastern diet is lentils, which contain a power-house of nutrients. This dish combines lentils with feta cheese to make a more complete protein and a very hearty entrée, as well as a dish bursting with the flavors of savory and sweet spices.*

*If you have access to a specialty store that deals in Mediterranean foods, try using either red or yellow lentils for additional color in the dish. If this is not possible, the common brown lentil is available in supermarkets.*

**Preparation Time: I hour** ▪ **Cooking Time: I hour** ▪ **Makes 6 servings**

▪ ▪ ▪

1½ cups finely chopped onions

2½ cups water

2 cups dried lentils, rinsed well

1 to 2 cloves garlic, minced

½ teaspoon ground cinnamon

½ teaspoon ground cumin

¼ teaspoon ground ginger

2 cups vegetable broth

1 carrot, peeled, halved lengthwise, and sliced

½ pound spinach leaves, cleaned and stems removed

2 cups chopped, seeded, peeled fresh tomatoes

Salt and freshly ground black pepper, to taste

1 cup crumbled feta cheese

1. In a large skillet, cook the onions and ½ cup water over medium-high heat for 5 to 8 minutes, until the onions are soft.

2. Add the lentils, garlic, cinnamon, cumin, ginger, broth, and remaining 2 cups water. Bring to a boil and reduce the heat to low. Cover and cook for 15 minutes.

3. Add the carrot. Re-cover and simmer for about 30 minutes, until the lentils are tender. The liquid should be almost absorbed, and the mixture should not be soupy.

4. Just before serving, add the spinach leaves and tomatoes and cook for 1 minute, until the spinach has wilted. Season with salt and pepper.

5. Sprinkle each serving with the feta. Serve hot.

# Persian Potatoes and Rice

*Children and adults alike scramble to be served a piece of the golden, crunchy potato that lines the skillet in this classic Middle Eastern rice dish commonly served at family and social gatherings. I must admit, I, too, have jockeyed to be toward the front of the line! Serve this rice dish under or to the side of the Mediterranean Vegetable Strata (page 138).*

**Preparation Time: 20 minutes ▪ Cooking Time: 1 hour ▪ Makes 6 to 8 servings**

▪ ▪ ▪

> 1 cup cold water
> 1½ cups white basmati rice, rinsed
> ¾ teaspoon salt
> 5 tablespoons butter
> 2 to 3 tablespoons grapeseed or extra-virgin olive oil
> 5 to 6 medium red potatoes, peeled and cut into ¼-inch-thick slices
> 1½ cups hot water

1. In a large pot, bring 1 cup cold water to a boil. Add the rice, salt, and 3 tablespoons butter and bring to a boil again. Reduce the heat to low. Cover and simmer for 10 to 15 minutes, until the rice is not completely soft. Set aside.

2. In a large skillet with a lid, heat the oil over medium-high heat. Arrange the sliced potatoes to cover the bottom of the skillet. Spoon the rice over the potatoes and cover the skillet. Cook over medium heat for 10 minutes.

3. Mix the 1½ cups hot water and the remaining 2 tablespoons butter together and pour this evenly over the rice. Reduce the heat to low. Cover and cook for 20 to 30 minutes, until the rice is fluffy and the potatoes are golden and crunchy on the bottom.

4. Serve hot.

# Sautéed Cabbage with Shallots and Lime

*Fresh greens are at the heart of the Southeast Asian diet. The presence of these fresh foods is everywhere, with people growing, picking, carrying, cooking, bartering, buying, and eating them. Small garden patches are seen everywhere, supplying the great demand for cabbages, mint, mustard greens, lime leaves, curry leaves, and more. In this sautéed dish, the flavors of shallots, sesame oil, garlic, and lime juice add a wonderful zest to the flavors of the common cabbage.*

**Preparation Time: 15 minutes ▪ Cooking Time: 15 minutes ▪ Makes 6 servings**

▪ ▪ ▪

> 2 shallots, finely chopped
>
> ¼ cup water
>
> 1 small head Savoy cabbage, quartered, cored, and thinly sliced
>
> 1 tablespoon minced garlic
>
> 2 tablespoons soy sauce
>
> 1 teaspoon sesame oil
>
> 2 tablespoons fresh lime juice

1. In a large skillet, cook the shallots and water over medium heat for about 2 minutes, until the shallots are tender.

2. Add all the remaining ingredients. Cook, stirring, for 8 to 10 minutes, until the cabbage is tender.

3. Taste for seasonings and add more soy sauce if needed. Serve hot.

# Stir-Fried Gingered Long Beans

*There is a special intensity to the flavor of the long bean, which is in the green bean family. When these delectable beans are paired with garlic, ginger, and sesame oil, you have a simple yet impressive side dish.*

*If you cannot find long beans at an Asian market or farmers' market, use any fresh green beans that are in season. In the winter months, frozen green beans can even be used with good results.*

**Preparation Time: 20 minutes ▪ Cooking Time: 10 minutes ▪ Makes 4 to 6 servings**

▪ ▪ ▪

> 1 tablespoon plus 1 teaspoon peanut oil with 10 to 12 drops sesame oil added
>
> 1 tablespoon minced garlic
>
> 1 pound long or green beans, cut into 4-inch lengths
>
> 1 teaspoon grated fresh ginger
>
> 2 teaspoons hoisin sauce
>
> 1 tablespoon soy sauce
>
> ½ cup water

1. In a large skillet with a lid, heat the oil over medium-high heat. Add the garlic and cook, stirring quickly, for a few seconds.

2. Add the long beans, ginger, hoisin sauce, soy sauce, and water. Cover the skillet, reduce the heat to low, and simmer for about 8 minutes, until the beans are tender.

3. Remove the lid, increase the heat to medium-high, and reduce any remaining liquid to the consistency of syrup.

# Squash with Ginger and Maple Syrup

*What child won't eat squash if you just sweeten the pot a little bit? Ginger, maple syrup, and lime juice help this simple squash recipe go down as easily as a sweet potato pie.*

**Preparation Time: 15 minutes** ▪ **Cooking Time: 1 hour** ▪ **Makes 4 servings**

▪ ▪ ▪

| | |
|---|---|
| 2 large winter squash or sweet potatoes | Salt, to taste |
| 2 tablespoons finely grated fresh ginger | Vegetable broth |
| 4 tablespoons butter | 3 tablespoons pure maple syrup |
| | Juice of ½ lime |

1. Preheat the oven to 350F (180C). If using winter squash, cut in half and scoop out the seeds. Place them, cut side down, on a baking sheet and bake for 30 to 45 minutes, depending on the size. If using sweet potatoes, bake them whole for 30 to 45 minutes. When done, scoop the squash or potatoes from the skins and place in a bowl.

2. In a small skillet, cook the ginger and butter over medium-low heat for 1 to 2 minutes.

3. Pour the ginger through a strainer, and reserve the butter and the ginger separately.

4. Add the ginger to the squash and mash well. Season with salt.

5. Add enough vegetable broth to the squash to reach the desired "mashed" texture.

6. Serve the squash in ½ cup portions. Make a well in the center of the mound on each individual plate. Pour equal portions of the reserved ginger butter into each of the wells.

7. Combine the maple syrup and lime juice. Pour equal portions of this mixture into each well along with the ginger butter. Serve hot.

# *Black-Eyed Peas with Sweet Peppers*

*Black-eyed peas are not only consumed to ring in a year of prosperity on New Year's Day, but are also very high in dietary fiber and folate. Thus, plates of black-eyed peas would be well placed in front of pregnant women, as they have a high demand for this immune-boosting, blood-building nutrient.*

**Preparation Time: 10 minutes • Cooking Time: 1 hour • Makes 4 servings**

■ ■ ■

> 1 onion, chopped
>
> 3 tablespoons water
>
> 4 cups vegetable broth
>
> 1½ cups dried black-eyed peas
>
> Salt, to taste
>
> 1 red bell pepper, roasted, peeled, and chopped (page 87)
>
> 1 green bell pepper, roasted, peeled, and chopped (page 87)

1. In a small skillet, cook the onion and water over medium heat for 3 to 5 minutes, until the onion is softened. Set aside.

2. In a large saucepan, combine the vegetable broth and black-eyed peas. Bring to a boil and reduce the heat to low. Cover and simmer for about 1 hour, until the peas are tender. Add additional water during the cooking if all of the liquid evaporates.

3. Just before serving, add the salt, onion, and red and green bell peppers.

## Black-Eyed Peas

It's thought that the black-eyed pea was brought to the United States through the African slave trade. Also called the cowpea, the small, kidney-shape bean is thought to have originated in Asia as long as three thousand years ago. It was also a staple of the Greek and Roman diets. Today, however, the bean is the center of attention at the New Year's Day table in Southern tables in the form of hoppin' John. Hoppin' John is black-eyed peas cooked with pork sausage, onion, garlic, pepper flakes, and rice. Though I didn't include a recipe for hoppin' John in the book, a vegetarian version can be made by substituting the sausage with vegetarian breakfast links, which can be found in the frozen foods section of the supermarket.

As for how Hoppin' John got its name, some say it was from the casual invitation of "Hop in, John!" Others say it came from the New Year's Day tradition in which the children hopped around the house once before eating the dish.

# *Cheesy Grits with Pecans*

*Now, some of you would say grits are an acquired taste if you weren't raised in the South, where grits may be served for breakfast, lunch, and dinner. However, once you add pecans and fontina cheese to this ground corn, you may find it takes no time at all to acquire the taste!*

**Preparation Time: 10 minutes ▪ Cooking Time: 15 minutes ▪ Makes 6 servings**

▪ ▪ ▪

1 large shallot, finely minced
4¼ cups water
1 cup milk
¾ teaspoon salt
1 cup grits
1½ cups grated fontina cheese
½ cup pecans, toasted

1. In a medium skillet, cook the shallot and ¼ cup water over medium heat for 3 to 5 minutes, until the shallot is soft.

2. Add the remaining 4 cups water, milk, salt, and grits. Stir well. Bring to a boil, stirring constantly. Reduce the heat to low and simmer for 10 to 12 minutes, until the grits reach a smooth, creamy texture, stirring occasionally.

3. Add the cheese and stir well until melted. Garnish with the pecans. Serve hot.

# Polenta with Smoked Cheddar

*As I have often said, each culture's cuisine has its own rib-sticking comfort foods. In the American South, it's grits; in Mexican-influenced cuisine, it's the masa that is made into tamales and tortillas; and in Italian cuisine, it's polenta.*

*Nothing could be easier than making polenta, as it's made the same as any other type of mush or hot cereal. It's the possibility of what can be added to it that makes polenta interesting to play with. Here, we turn to the French tradition of shallots as the base flavor, then add jalapeños, and finally smoked Cheddar cheese to infuse the flavors of the Southwest.*

*For making a quick, firm-style grilled polenta accompaniment to a dish, you can find polenta in premade loafs in many supermarkets; just slice, heat, and serve.*

**Preparation Time: 10 minutes ▪ Cooking Time: 15 to 20 minutes ▪ Makes 4 to 6 servings**

▪ ▪ ▪

| | |
|---|---|
| ¼ cup finely chopped shallots | 4 cups water |
| 1 tablespoon finely chopped jalapeño chile | 1 cup polenta |
| Pinch cayenne pepper | 1 teaspoon salt |
| ½ tablespoon butter | 1½ cups grated smoked Cheddar cheese |

1. In a small skillet, cook the shallots, jalapeño, and cayenne in the butter over medium heat for 3 to 4 minutes.

2. In a large saucepan, bring the water to a boil and stir in the polenta and salt. Bring to a boil again, stirring constantly. Reduce the heat and cook at a low boil for 15 to 20 minutes, until the polenta thickens and the grains of corn are thoroughly cooked. Add small amounts of water if the mixture becomes too dry; you want a smooth and creamy texture.

3. When the polenta is cooked, stir in the shallot mixture and the cheese. Stir until the cheese has melted. Remove from the heat and serve hot.

*chilies*

■ ■ ■

# Southwestern Succotash

*In the classic understanding of the word, succotash is a combination of sweet corn kernels and lima beans with perhaps a little butter and salt. That's not what we're doing here. Although I enjoy the combination of corn and beans, I prefer a dish to have a little more going on, so I've added Anaheim and jalapeños chilies, tomatillos, and chili powder to liven it up a bit. You choose the bean.*

**Preparation Time: 15 minutes ▪ Cooking Time: 8 to 10 minutes ▪ Makes 4 servings**

■ ■ ■

3 tablespoons butter or olive oil

2 Anaheim or poblano chilies, quartered, seeded, and sliced ¼ inch thick

2 ears fresh corn, kernels cut off

2 large tomatillos, chopped

2 crookneck squash, sliced ¼ to ½ inch thick

1½ cups cooked beans (your favorite variety)

Salt and freshly ground black pepper, to taste

2 teaspoons finely minced jalapeño chili (optional)

1 teaspoon chili powder

½ cup vegetable broth

2 teaspoons finely chopped fresh oregano

1 small avocado, pitted and diced

1. Heat the butter in a large skillet over medium-high heat.

2. Add the Anaheim chilies, corn, and tomatillos. Cook for 1 to 2 minutes.

3. Add the squash, beans, salt, pepper, jalapeño, chili powder, and broth. Cook for 1 to 2 minutes, until the vegetables are crisp-tender.

4. Stir in the oregano and remove from the heat.

5. Stir in the avocado and serve hot.

# DESSERTS
*Life Is Sweet—Indulge!*

■ ■ ■

Our desire for the sweetness in life extends to all the senses. And why not?

The scent of peaches, vanilla, cinnamon, and chocolate takes us from recognition to desire, filling us with anticipation, pleasure, and comfort.

The taste of sweet was once our survival as Mother Earth seldom, if ever, offered our ancestors sweet foods that were not safe. Bitter could lead to death; sweet was safe.

Is it a wonder then that every culture on the planet reserves a soft spot for sweets?

In the following pages you will experience sweets from around the world with as simple a pleasure as Stuffed Figs in Chocolate to a Lime Tart with Tequila, tangy and billowing with whipped cream. Although some of the desserts have a low-fat content, I do not view dessert as an inherent sin. Therefore, some of the desserts would indeed be considered decadent, as I believe there is a time and place for all things, unless an unbalanced state of health does not allow for such extravagances. I would not consume a rich dessert on a daily basis, but a dish of Café Gelato and a Pecan Florentine make a scrumptious occasional indulgence.

Ideally, you would begin with only the freshest ingredients, including fresh dairy products where they are called for. In addition, I have switched to organic for milk, butter, sour cream, and cottage cheese, and I like to use free-range eggs. This reduces the load of antibiotics, hormones, herbicides, and insecticides passed on to humans through the cow milk and eggs of chickens raised on nonorganic products. Goat milk products are also an option, as some people have an easier time digesting goat milk. Another option is to avoid dairy altogether by using almond, soy, or rice milks and creams, and margarines that do not contain trans-fatty acids. Egg replacer can also be used instead of eggs.

For the same reasons, I try to use organic flours, readily available in most natural food stores. The same is true with sugars and syrups.

It's also a good idea to invest in a quality vanilla extract such as a Madagascar bourbon vanilla. The flavor is decidedly better.

Go ahead, no one's looking—indulge!

# Mango and Sautéed Bananas with Honey, Lime, and Yogurt

*These tropical fruits need no adornment for daily consumption. However, a little special treatment, such as the honey and yogurt in this recipe, is in order for special occasions. Here, you can taste the sunshine, as a tart, sweet and creamy yogurt dressing tops mango and sautéed bananas in this light summer salad or dessert.*

**Preparation Time: 20 minutes ▪ Cooking Time: 5 minutes ▪ Makes 2 servings**

1 cup nonfat plain yogurt

¼ cup honey

2 tablespoons fresh lime juice

2 bananas, sliced lengthwise and halved

1 tablespoon unsalted butter

1 mango, cubed (page 197)

1. In a small bowl, combine the yogurt, honey, and lime juice and set aside.

2. In a medium skillet, sauté the bananas in the butter over medium heat for about 5 minutes, until they begin to brown. Place 2 banana halves on each plate.

3. Surround the bananas with some of the cubed mango, spoon the yogurt sauce over the top, and serve.

# Mangos

This fragrant and exotic fruit was originally cultivated in India, but it is being grown in many parts of the world today. Depending on the variety of mango, they can range from 6 ounces to 4 pounds in size. The skin of a ripe mango should be smooth with a beautiful deep-yellow color mottled with red. The flesh is a brilliant orange, contains lots of juice, and has a wonderful sweet and tart flavor. The only problematic aspect of dealing with mangos is the oversize seed, which runs the length of the fruit. After removing the skin, delicately cut the flesh away from the seed with a sharp paring knife.

Green mangos are also used in cooking, but mostly in Indian and Southeast Asian cuisine as a tart complement to vegetable dishes, as well as for pickling and seasoning. For most purposes, you want to use the golden ripe mango.

This ripe fruit is so succulent that it needs no adornment. It's wonderful when eaten by itself or used in desserts, salads, salsas, and chutney.

# Gingerbread with Lemon Sauce

*Gingerbread with lemon sauce conjures up more associations with comfort food than just about any other recipe for my sister, Denise, and me. We would wait at the oven door for our mother's fresh, hot gingerbread to emerge. With the gingerbread steaming hot on the plate, the wait became almost unbearable while Mom ladled the hot lemon sauce over the spicy, dark cake. I hope this recipe brings such sweet feelings for you and your loved ones.*

**Preparation Time: 30 minutes** ▪ **Cooking Time: 60 minutes** ▪ **Makes 8 servings**

**GINGERBREAD**

$2\frac{1}{2}$ cups all-purpose flour

1 teaspoon ground cinnamon

1 teaspoon ground cloves

2 teaspoons ground ginger

$\frac{1}{2}$ teaspoon hickory salt, or $\frac{1}{2}$ teaspoon liquid smoke plus rounded $\frac{1}{4}$ teaspoon salt

$\frac{1}{2}$ cup (8 tablespoons) unsalted butter, softened

$\frac{1}{2}$ cup packed dark brown sugar

1 cup dark molasses

2 teaspoons baking soda

1 cup boiling water

2 large eggs, lightly beaten

$\frac{1}{2}$ cup chopped candied ginger

**LEMON SAUCE**

$\frac{1}{2}$ cup fresh lemon juice

$1\frac{1}{2}$ cups confectioners' sugar

Pinch salt

1. To make the Gingerbread: Preheat the oven to 350F (180C). Grease and flour an 8-inch-square baking pan.

2. Sift the flour, cinnamon, cloves, ginger, and hickory salt into a bowl and set aside. (If using liquid smoke, add it to the butter mixture in step 4 with the salt.)

3. In a mixing bowl, beat together the butter and brown sugar until creamy. Add the molasses and beat until smooth.

4. In a small bowl, combine the baking soda and boiling water and add to the butter mixture. Mix well. Add the flour mixture, mix well, and then beat in the eggs. Stir in the candied ginger.

5. Pour the batter into the pan and bake for 45 to 55 minutes, or until a toothpick inserted into the center comes out clean.

6. Remove from the oven. Cool in the pan for 10 minutes. Cut into squares.

7. While the gingerbread is cooling, prepare the Lemon Sauce: Combine the lemon juice, confectioners' sugar, and salt in a saucepan and whisk over low heat until the sugar is dissolved.

8. Transfer the gingerbread squares to dessert plates. Spoon the lemon sauce over the warm gingerbread.

# Candied Ginger Cookies

Although the Chinese don't have the West's obsession for sweet pastries, chocolates, and cakes, small cookies are often served with tea. In keeping with the flavors of the East, we've created a ginger-based cookie. Here, we've expanded on the ginger theme with the addition of pieces of crystallized ginger, to make a mouth-watering cookie that can be served with any hot beverage from Chinese teas to French roast coffee.

**Preparation Time: 30 minutes ▪ Cooking Time: 10 to 12 minutes ▪ Makes 3 dozen**

▪ ▪ ▪

¾ cup (12 tablespoons) unsalted butter, softened

1 cup sugar plus ½ cup for rolling cookies

1 large egg

¼ cup molasses

2 cups all-purpose flour

2 teaspoons baking soda

½ teaspoon salt

1 tablespoon ground ginger

1 teaspoon Chinese five-spice powder

½ cup chopped candied ginger

1. Preheat the oven to 350F (180C). Grease a baking sheet or line it with parchment paper.

2. In a mixing bowl, beat the butter until smooth. Add the 1 cup sugar and beat until creamy. Add the egg and beat until fluffy. Beat in the molasses.

3. In another bowl, stir together the flour, baking soda, salt, ground ginger, and five-spice powder. Add the dry ingredients to the butter mixture, beating until smooth and blended. Stir in the candied ginger until evenly distributed.

4. Form the dough into 1-inch balls. Roll them in the ½ cup sugar and place them about 2 inches apart on the prepared baking sheet. Bake for 10 to 12 minutes, until the cookies have spread and the tops have cracked. Transfer the baking sheet to a wire rack and cool for 10 minutes before removing the cookies.

# Sour Cherry Cobbler with Sour Cream

*Ah, how many of us are taken back to late spring/early summer when the cherries begin to appear at produce stands in the northern hemisphere? Because summers are short and winters long, Eastern European cooks have a long history of canning the season's bounty for the harsher months ahead. Sour cherries are among the fruits that are commonly canned for future use, and there are few homier uses for sour cherries than a hot cobbler topped with a dollop of slightly sweetened sour cream.*

**Preparation Time: 30 minutes** ▪ **Cooking Time: 40 minutes** ▪ **Makes 6 servings**

▪ ▪ ▪

### FILLING
3 tablespoons all-purpose flour

¾ cup sugar (if the cherries are packed in syrup, use only ¼ cup sugar)

4 cups canned sour cherries, drained

### CRUST
1 cup all-purpose flour

1 teaspoon baking powder

½ teaspoon salt

6 tablespoons unsalted butter, chilled

¼ cup whipping cream

About 1 tablespoon milk

1 teaspoon sugar

### TOPPING
¾ cup sour cream

1 teaspoon pure vanilla extract

2 tablespoons sugar

1. Preheat the oven to 375F (190C). To make the filling: Combine the flour and the sugar in a bowl. Add the cherries, mix, and spoon into a baking dish deep enough for the fruit and the crust (about 1½ quarts).

2. To make the crust: Mix the flour, baking powder, and salt in a food processor.

3. Cut the butter into small cubes and add to the dry ingredients. Process until the butter is in pea-size pieces.

4. Add the cream and process until the dough is soft and crumbly. Remove the dough from the food processor and press it together with your hands.

5. On a lightly floured board, roll out the dough with a floured rolling pin until it is the size of your baking dish. Carefully lift it onto the top of the fruit. Tuck the edges into the sides of the baking dish, if necessary. The dough does not need to appear smooth on the top.

6. Brush the top of the dough lightly with milk and sprinkle with sugar. Make a few slashes in the top of the dough to let the steam escape.

7. Bake for about 40 minutes, until the top is brown and the fruit is bubbling.

8. To make the topping: In a small bowl, mix the sour cream with the vanilla and sugar.

9. Spoon the warm cobbler into dessert bowls and top each serving with a dollop of sour cream.

# Vanilla Extract

In times past, girls would secretly tip a bottle of vanilla onto a finger and dab a little of the sweet, intoxicating aroma behind their ears before seeing their sweetheart. Today, women spend big dollars on lotions, creams, candles, and room sprays scented by America's favorite aroma. Because it's indispensable in the kitchen of any home baker, I thought it worth a word or two on vanilla extract.

First, it's important to purchase the real, pure vanilla extract instead of vanilla flavoring. A small amount of pure extract goes a long way and imparts a more intense aroma and flavor than that of its imposters. It's true that you have to pay more, but consider what it takes to produce real vanilla extract.

The following is the process Baldwin Extracts uses to make their famous vanilla extract. First the Madagascar vanilla beans, called bourbon beans (no relation to the alcohol), spend a year on the vine before they reach maturity. The beans are picked and dried through a natural sun-drying process. From here, the beans are stored in the dark until they travel as much as halfway around the world to reach their destination. The chopped beans are then suspended in a fine-mesh strainer suspended in a percolator. Ethyl alcohol and water are added to the beans, and they are left to stew for 5 days. The liquid is then drained into jugs and the contents poured through a strainer and into an oak barrel. The rich, dark liquid is stirred and left to sit for 2 days. At this point, the liquid is drained again and emptied into another oak barrel, where it cures for another 2 weeks. The finished vanilla extract is drained into quart-size bottles. Some is sent off to be tested by the Federal Bureau of Alcohol, Tobacco and Firearms (it's true!) to ensure a 35 percent alcohol level, then it's poured into retail-size bottles. And with all that, the Baldwins still charge just over $1 an ounce. You can look Baldwin Extracts up on the Internet for more information.

Vanilla is also available in syrup and powder form for baking.

# Apple and Sesame Tart Tatin

*I made it my mission to find the best tart tatin during a visit to France. I ordered it at one bistro and café after another. As it turned out, I discovered this version years later at a café in Vancouver, B.C., and found it to rival the best of them! The use of puff pastry and freshness of the presentation give it a little je 'ne sais quoi.*

**Preparation Time: 30 to 40 minutes** ▪ **Cooking Time: 30 minutes** ▪ **Makes 4 servings**
▪ ▪ ▪

2 large apples, peeled and thinly sliced
4 tablespoons butter
2 tablespoons brandy
1 teaspoon sesame seeds
¼ cup packed light brown sugar
1 pound purchased puff pastry

1. Preheat the oven to 400F (205C). Place the apples, butter, and brandy in an oven-proof skillet and cook over medium-high heat for 5 minutes.

2. Sprinkle with the sesame seeds and brown sugar. Cook for another 2 minutes.

3. Roll the pastry out on a lightly floured board. Trim with a knife into the shape of your skillet. Cover the apples with the puff pastry.

4. Bake for 25 minutes, until the pastry is brown.

5. Remove the skillet from the oven. Place it over medium heat and cook for another few minutes until the apple mixture is caramelized and the juices have thickened. Turn out onto a plate and cut into quarters. Serve hot.

## *Baklava*

The juice and zest of fresh oranges gives this version of baklava a particularly lovely and delicate flavor.

The reason the recipe is so large is that if you're going to go to the trouble of making this exquisite dessert, you might as well make enough to share!

**Preparation Time: I hour** ▪ **Cooking Time: 30 minutes** ▪ **Makes 24 pieces**

▪ ▪ ▪

> 2 cups finely chopped walnuts
> Zest of 2 oranges, very finely chopped
> 2 tablespoons plus ¼ cup sugar
> 1 teaspoon ground cinnamon
> Pinch ground cloves
> Pinch ground allspice
> ¼ cup honey
> Juice of 2 oranges plus enough water to make a total of ¾ cup
> 2 tablespoons fresh lemon juice
> Pinch salt
> 16-ounce package phyllo (thaw overnight in the refrigerator, if frozen)
> ¾ cup unsalted butter, melted

1. In a bowl, combine the walnuts, orange zest, 2 tablespoons sugar, cinnamon, cloves, and allspice. Set aside.

2. In a medium saucepan, mix the honey, ¼ cup sugar, orange juice, and lemon juice. Simmer over low heat until the mixture forms a syrup thick enough to coat the back of a spoon. Remove from the heat. Add the salt and pour into a bowl to cool.

3. Preheat the oven to 350F (180C). Butter a large baking sheet or cover it with a sheet of parchment paper. Remove the phyllo from the package and lay it flat next to the

baking sheet. Lay the sheets of dough, one at a time, on the baking sheet, brushing each sheet with melted butter. Continue until half the dough has been used (about 10 sheets).

4. Spread the nut mixture evenly over the layered phyllo. Place the remaining sheets of dough on top of the nut mixture, brushing each with butter, as before, until all the dough is used up.

5. Make diagonal, 2-inch diamond-shape cuts into the top layers of dough and filling, leaving the bottom layers of dough uncut.

6. Bake about 30 minutes. If not browned on the top, increase the temperature to 450F (230C) and bake for a few more minutes, until golden brown.

7. Pour the cooled syrup over the dough. Cut through the remaining bottom layers of the dough. Cool completely before serving.

# Cookie-and-Nut-Stuffed Peaches

Cibo di conforto, *is how you say "food of comfort" in Italian, although they really don't have a term for comfort food. This fresh peach dessert exemplifies the term and, I'll warn you, you might become addicted to this dessert during the summer peach season!*

**Preparation Time: 20 minutes** ▪ **Cooking Time: 25 minutes** ▪ **Makes 8 servings**

▪ ▪ ▪

> **4 medium peaches or nectarines**
>
> **1²/₃ cups cookie crumbs, such as gingersnaps, molasses cookies, or Bordeaux cookies**
>
> **¹/₂ cup finely chopped walnuts or pecans**
>
> **¹/₄ cup packed light brown sugar**
>
> **¹/₄ cup butter, softened**
>
> **Triple Sec**
>
> **Vanilla ice cream (optional)**

1. Preheat the oven to 400F (205C). Split each peach in half and carve the pit from the peaches. Spoon or cut out the flesh, leaving a ¹/₂-inch-thick shell. Place the shells on a baking sheet. Chop the peach flesh and place it in a bowl. Reserve some peach for 8 thin slices to use as a garnish.

2. Combine the peach flesh, cookie crumbs, nuts, brown sugar, and butter. Spoon equal portions of this mixture into each peach half. Drizzle Triple Sec over the top of each peach half.

3. Garnish the top of each piece with reserved peach slices. Bake for 20 to 25 minutes, until topping is browned. Serve hot with vanilla ice cream (if using) or allow them to cool to room temperature and serve plain.

# Exotic Almond Cookies

*These cookies are an exotic version of peanut butter cookies. They lasted only minutes when I put a trayful in front of the children at a family gathering. In fact, I dare you to eat just one!*

**Time: 20 minutes ▪ Cooking Time: 15 minutes ▪ Makes 2 dozen**

▪ ▪ ▪

> ¾ cup (12 tablespoons) salted butter, softened
> ¼ cup tahini paste (page 13)
> ¾ cup sugar
> 1 teaspoon pure vanilla extract
> 1 egg yolk
> 1¾ cups all-purpose flour
> ½ teaspoon salt
> 24 whole blanched almonds

1. Preheat the oven to 375F (190C). Line a baking sheet with parchment paper or use a nonstick one. In a large bowl, cream together the butter, tahini, and sugar.

2. Add the vanilla and egg yolk. Beat until smooth.

3. Stir in the flour and salt (the mixture will be dry).

4. With your hands, form the dough into walnut-size balls and place them on the prepared baking sheet.

5. Press an almond into the center of each cookie.

6. Bake for 13 to 14 minutes, until the cookies turn golden brown. Cool on the baking sheet on a wire rack.

# Sautéed Bananas and Rum

*Downright sinful, but worth the guilt!*

**Preparation Time: 10 minutes ▪ Cooking Time: 5 minutes ▪ Makes 4 servings**

**2 to 4 tablespoons unsalted butter**

**4 small bananas, sliced**

**5 tablespoons light brown sugar**

**4 tablespoons rum or bourbon**

**Vanilla or chocolate ice cream**

1. In a large skillet, melt the butter over medium-high heat. Add the bananas and cook for 30 to 40 seconds.

2. Add the brown sugar and cook, stirring, until bubbly.

3. Add the rum and cook for 30 seconds, stirring, until the liquid has evaporated.

4. Serve hot over vanilla or chocolate ice cream.

# *Lime Sherbet with White Chocolate*

*If you can't afford to sin to the scale of the Sautéed Bananas and Rum (page 209) over ice cream, this will be certain to tingle your taste buds! Fresh lime juice and white chocolate combine to make one of the most intriguing sherbets I've experienced. It also serves to cool off the palate after a filling and heat-filled Mexican meal.*

**Preparation Time: 30 minutes** ▪ **Cooking Time: 0** ▪ **Makes I pint**

▪ ▪ ▪

> ½ cup fresh lemon and lime juices (about 2 parts lemon to 1 part lime)
> ½ cup sugar
> 1 cup milk
> ½ teaspoon pure vanilla extract
> ½ cup half-and-half
> Zest of 1 lime
> 3 drops green food coloring (optional)
> ¼ cup shredded or grated white chocolate

1. Combine all the ingredients and freeze according to the ice-cream maker's instructions.

2. Serve immediately or pack into a freezer container and freeze for a firmer consistency.

# *Lemon Buttermilk Sherbet*

*At the end of a rich and satisfying meal of legumes, cheeses, vegetables, savory spices, and herbs, this cool and refreshing sherbet of lemon juice and buttermilk is the perfect palate refresher. It can be served alone or with a light drizzle of the lemon sauce that accompanies this recipe.*

**Preparation Time: 25 minutes** ▪ **Cooking Time: 15 minutes** ▪ **Makes 1 quart**

▪ ▪ ▪

| ZESTY LEMON SAUCE | LEMON BUTTERMILK SHERBET |
|---|---|
| ½ cup water | 1½ cups sugar |
| ½ cup sugar | ⅔ cup fresh lemon juice |
| Zest of 2 lemons, cut into strips | 1 quart buttermilk |
| 3 tablespoons half–and–half | 1 teaspoon pure vanilla extract |
| Pinch salt | Pinch salt |

1. To make the sauce: In a saucepan, cook the water, sugar, and lemon zest over medium heat for 12 to 13 minutes, until the liquid is reduced and thickened, golden in color, and bubbling. Remove the zest with a slotted spoon and discard.

2. Add the half-and-half and stir gently until the mixture returns to a foamy boil. Add salt, stir quickly, and remove from the heat.

3. Pour into a heatproof container and refrigerate until chilled.

4. Meanwhile, to make the sherbet: Dissolve the sugar in the lemon juice. Stir in the buttermilk, vanilla extract, and salt and freeze according to the ice-cream maker's instructions.

5. To serve, drizzle a spoonful of the sauce over each serving of the lemon-buttermilk sherbet.

# *Stuffed Figs in Chocolate*

*This intensely flavored natural little dessert goes well with Turkish coffee. Both are served in small portions but are very rich and satisfying. If you cannot find figs, dates can be used.*

**Preparation Time: 20 to 30 minutes** ▪ **Cooking Time: 10 minutes** ▪ **Makes 12 pieces**

▪ ▪ ▪

> **12 dried Mission or Calimyrna figs**
> **12 walnut halves or whole almonds**
> **8 ounces semisweet chocolate**

1. Using a sharp knife, split the figs in half, but do not cut all the way through, so that the fig halves remain attached on one side.

2. Place a walnut half inside each fig and press it closed.

3. Heat the chocolate in a double boiler over low heat, or in the microwave until it melts. (Do not overcook.)

4. One at a time, dip each of the figs into the melted chocolate, rolling it around until it is thoroughly coated with chocolate. (There will be chocolate left over, but extra is needed to allow for the final pieces to be rolled and thoroughly coated in the chocolate.) Remove the fig quickly from the chocolate with a fork or spoon and place it on a tray. Allow the figs to cool until the chocolate is firm before serving.

# Figs

It's no surprise that the fig is still a mystery to many of us. Steeped in history and mythology, the fig represents sensuality and the sins of the flesh. Its sticky and seed-filled flesh confounds the uninitiated palate, but this is a journey well worth embarking upon.

Figs date back 5,000 years to the eastern shores of the Mediterranean and deep into the Middle Eastern countries. Pliny the Elder, of the first century A.D. declared figs as a healer of feebleness and important in keeping skin free of wrinkles. As the fig migrated to other parts of Asia, it became popular as a sweetener. Finally, the fig made its way to California along with the missionaries, thus the variety known as Mission figs. California's warm and dry climate created an ideal growing environment for the fig, allowing it to become more readily available to the Western world.

Today, 20 percent of the world's dry fig production comes from California.

But aside from Fig Newtons in the lunchbox, many of us have had little experience with using figs in the diet. Even fewer have experienced the delight of a succulent fresh fig on the tongue, an experience that nearly brings a blush to the cheeks.

## Fig Facts

Rich in complex carbohydrates.

Good source of dietary fiber.

Rich in essential minerals such as potassium, iron, and calcium.

Contain no fat, cholesterol, or sodium.

Storage is best in a cool, dry place.

Can be frozen with excellent results.

## Recipe Notes

Try fresh or dried figs in salads along with a sharp or tangy cheese, fresh greens, and a light vinaigrette dressing with a mild-flavored oil at the base.

*Coconut*

## Coconut Custard

*Every cuisine has its comforting foods, and this Coconut Custard recipe might reign supreme as such a dish in Southeast Asia. The creaminess and richness of the custard and the sweet, chewy quality of shredded coconut impart an undeniable sensuality to this ethnic custard dish.*

**Preparation Time: 20 minutes ▪ Cooking Time: 45 minutes ▪ Makes 6 servings**

▪ ▪ ▪

3 eggs

2 egg yolks

½ cup sugar

Pinch salt

1¼ cups milk, heated until hot

1 (14-ounce) can coconut milk (unsweetened)

1 teaspoon pure vanilla extract

¾ cup unsweetened shredded coconut

1. Preheat the oven to 325F (165C). Butter a 1-quart soufflé dish or 6 ramekins.

2. Beat the eggs and egg yolks together in a bowl until light. Add the sugar and salt and mix well. Add the hot milk slowly, stirring constantly. Add the coconut milk, vanilla, and coconut. Mix well and pour into the soufflé dish.

3. Place a shallow pan, large enough to hold the soufflé dish, in your oven. Fill the pan with hot water and place the soufflé dish in the pan. This prevents the formation of a leathery crust on the custard.

4. Bake for 40 to 45 minutes, until the custard is set. The custard is set when a knife inserted in the center comes out clean. Remove from the water bath and cool.

# Honeydew Sorbet with Lime Juice

*This melon sorbet is so light and clean that it can be served as a palate cleanser between courses as well as for a petite and refreshing dessert.*

**Preparation Time: 10 minutes** ▪ **Cooking Time: 0** ▪ **Makes 1 pint**

▪ ▪ ▪

> ½ **cup sugar**
> **Juice of 1 to 1½ limes**
> **1 honeydew melon**

1. In a bowl, dissolve the sugar in the lime juice.

2. Cut the melon into cubes and place it in a food processor. Puree the melon first using a food processor then transferring to a blender.

3. Add the lime juice mixture. Freeze the sorbet according to the ice-cream maker's instructions.

# *Fruit Soup with Sabayon*

*This delicate, fresh dessert was inspired by the same dish made by John Ash, author of* From the Earth to the Table *(Dutton, 1995), on one of my cooking shows. A fabulous chef and gentleman, I joined him in his kitchen for the videotaping, and the recipe was so outstanding I couldn't pass up the opportunity to share the recipe with you.*

**Preparation Time: 30 minutes ■ Cooking Time: 10 minutes ■ Makes 4 servings**

■ ■ ■

**SABAYON**
1 egg
2 egg yolks
Pinch salt
⅔ cup sweet dessert wine
½ cup sugar

2 fresh peaches, peeled and cut into cubes
2 to 3 assorted fresh berries
1 tablespoon sugar
2 cups fresh or frozen raspberries, pureed in the blender and strained through a fine-mesh strainer to remove the seeds

1. To make the Sabayon: In the top of a double boiler over medium heat, whisk together the egg, yolks, salt, wine, and sugar over low-simmering water, stirring constantly, until the mixture becomes thick, foamy, and warm to the touch. Do not let it simmer, or you will scramble the eggs. It must, however, heat through in order to thicken.

2. Arrange the peaches and assorted berries on individual plates.

3. In a bowl, mix the sugar and raspberry puree and drizzle it over the fruit. Top each portion with about 2 tablespoons sabayon and serve warm or cold.

# Lemon Cheesecake with Gingersnap Crust

*Although many of us were raised with the thick, creamy-style cheesecake, I have learned to love a lighter version. It has more the consistency of Jewish cheesecake due to the use of ricotta, rather than cream cheese. We have also substituted a light version of sour cream for the regular to help take some of the guilt out of this ordinarily fat-laden favorite. Gingersnaps definitely give a snap to the finished product.*

**Preparation Time: 30 minutes** ▪ **Cooking Time: 1 hour, 15 minutes** ▪ **Makes 8 servings**

▪ ▪ ▪

**FILLING**

2 cups ricotta cheese

1½ cups light sour cream

4 eggs

2 tablespoons all-purpose flour

1 cup sugar

½ teaspoon pure almond extract

½ teaspoon pure vanilla extract (optional)

Grated zest of 2 lemons

**GINGERSNAP CRUST**

1 cup crushed gingersnap cookies

3 tablespoons butter, softened

3 tablespoons sugar

**TO SERVE (OPTIONAL)**

Fresh berries of choice

Sugar, to taste

1. To make the filling: In a small bowl, mix the ricotta cheese and sour cream together. Place this mixture in a fine-mesh strainer over a bowl and allow it to drain for 45 minutes. Transfer the cheese mixture to a food processor.

2. Add the eggs, flour, sugar, almond and vanilla extracts, and lemon zest to the ricotta mixture in the food processor and pulse for a few seconds, until the mixture is smooth.

3. Meanwhile, to make the crust: Preheat the oven to 350F (180C). Mix the gingersnap crumbs, butter, and sugar together in a bowl. Press this mixture into the bottom of an 8-inch springform pan. Bake for 5 to 6 minutes. Remove from the oven. Let cool. Reduce the oven temperature to 325F (165C).

4. Pour the ricotta mixture over the crust and bake for 1 hour, 15 minutes. Remove from the oven. Cool by chilling in the refrigerator for 3 to 4 hours or overnight.

5. Remove the side of the pan. Serve plain or with berries that have been sprinkled with sugar.

### Café Gelato

*The simple truth is that there is no way to finish a true Cajun or Creole meal without overindulging. So go ahead, and enjoy this delectable gelato at the end of the meal. You might even want to scoop up some with one of the Pecan Florentines (page 220). You can always fast tomorrow!*

**Preparation Time: 30 minutes ▪ Cooking Time: 10 to 15 minutes ▪ Makes 1 quart**

▪ ▪ ▪

2 cups half-and-half
3½ tablespoons instant coffee crystals dissolved in 2 tablespoons boiling water
4 egg yolks
¾ cup sugar (turbinado, if available)
1 teaspoon pure vanilla extract
1½ cups heavy cream

1. In a medium saucepan over medium heat, bring the half-and-half and coffee to just under a boil and remove from the stove.

2. In a bowl, whisk the egg yolks and sugar together until smooth. Gradually whisk into the coffee mixture and place the saucepan back over medium heat. Cook, stirring constantly, until the custard begins to thicken and coats the back of a wooden spoon.

3. Remove the pan from the heat. Add the vanilla and heavy cream.

4. Refrigerate for 4 to 6 hours, until well chilled. Freeze the gelato according to the ice-cream maker's instructions.

# Pecan Florentines

*I must tell you straight up that these Florentine cookies are the best I've ever had! I believe it's the addition of orange peel that sets them apart from the rest.*

**Preparation Time: 1 hour ■ Cooking Time: 7 to 9 minutes ■ Makes 12 cookies**

■ ■ ■

**ORANGE PEEL**
1 cup water
½ cup sugar
⅓ cup chopped orange peel

**COOKIE DOUGH**
⅔ cup plus 2 teaspoons confectioners' sugar
2 tablespoons sour cream
2 tablespoons dark rum
¾ cup sliced or chopped pecans
3 tablespoons all-purpose flour

4 ounces bittersweet chocolate

1. To candy the orange peel: Bring the water to a boil. Add the sugar and boil until the sugar dissolves. Add the orange peel, reduce the heat to medium-low, and simmer for about 10 minutes. Remove the peel from the syrup and drain on a piece of parchment paper until cool.

2. To make the cookie dough: Cover 2 baking sheets with parchment paper. Preheat the oven to 375F (190C).

3. In a large bowl, combine the sugar, sour cream, and rum and stir until smooth.

4. Add the pecans and candied orange peel and mix well. Sift the flour over the batter and stir it in.

5. For each cookie, spoon about 1 tablespoon batter onto the parchment-covered sheet, leaving 2 to 3 inches between each mound. Flatten each mound with a fork.

6. Bake, 1 sheet at a time, for 7 to 9 minutes, until the cookies have spread and browned around the edges but are still pale in the centers. Remove the cookies from the oven and let them cool on the baking sheet. When cooled, carefully peel the parchment paper off the cookies.

7. Melt the chocolate in the top of a double boiler over simmering water. With a knife, spread the underside of each cookie with the melted chocolate. Place each cookie, chocolate side up, on a wire rack and cool until the chocolate is solid. Store in an air-tight container.

# *pudding* ... ■
## *Bread Pudding*

*I have bragged about this bread pudding to friends and strangers alike through the years. The secret is the use of croissants rather than the French bread that's traditionally used. Croissants make for a much more delicate texture than the usual heaviness of bread pudding.*

*Serve it, sit back, and enjoy the raves.*

**Preparation Time: 20 minutes ■ Cooking Time: 1 hour ■ Makes 4 to 6 servings**

■ ■ ■

4 cups croissant pieces

¼ cup raisins

¼ cup toasted sliced almonds (optional)

1 cup milk

1¼ cups half-and-half, or fat-free evaporated milk for a lighter version

3 egg yolks

½ cup sugar

1 teaspoon pure vanilla extract

1 tablespoon bourbon (optional)

2 tablespoons butter, melted

1. Preheat the oven to 375F (190C). Place the croissants in an 8-inch-square baking dish.

2. Sprinkle the raisins and almonds (if using) evenly over the croissants.

3. In a bowl, beat the milk, half-and-half, and egg yolks until smooth. Add the sugar, vanilla, and bourbon (if using). Mix well and pour gently over the croissants. Do not stir.

4. Drizzle the butter over the top. Bake for about 1 hour, until the top is puffed and lightly browned.

5. Serve warm or at room temperature.

# *Lemon Sorbet in Lemon Cups*

*If you've already unbuckled your belt a notch after your comfortable Southern supper, you might want to finish it with a most refreshing little dessert.*

*I was introduced to these frozen citrus cups at the Renaissance Faire, which ran each year in the early fall when the temperatures were still spiking into the high 90s in the central valley of California. Nothing cooled us down faster than these little frozen confections served in their own natural skins.*

**Preparation Time: 30 minutes ▪ Cooking Time: 0 ▪ Makes 8 cups**

▪ ▪ ▪

> **6 lemons**
> **1½ to 2 cups pure maple syrup**
> **1 cup water**
> **¼ cup chopped fresh mint**
> **Mint leaves, for garnish**

1. Slice 4 lemons crosswise, juice them, and scoop out the remaining pulp with a melon baller or a spoon to clean what will become the "cups." Set these aside. Juice the remaining 2 lemons; you need 1¼ cups lemon juice.

2. In a bowl, mix the lemon juice, maple syrup, and water. Add the chopped mint and set it aside for 10 minutes.

3. Strain out the mint and discard. Freeze the juice mixture according to the ice-cream maker's instructions.

4. Cut a small slice from the bottom of each lemon half so it will sit flat on a plate.

5. When the sorbet is ready, fill each lemon "cup" with sorbet and garnish with fresh mint leaves.

6. Serve immediately or place them in the freezer until you are ready to serve.

## Lime Tart with Tequila

*If you enjoy a lime or lemon tart, I would encourage you to give this sublime citrus tart a try, which not only has the tart and creamy taste you would expect, but an extra-flavor bonus from the coconut and toasted hazelnuts buried in the crust.*

**Preparation Time: 1 hour ▪ Cooking Time: 20 minutes ▪ Makes 8 to 12 servings**

**CRUST**
¼ cup hazelnuts
1½ cups finely ground vanilla wafers
3 tablespoons unsweetened shredded coconut, toasted
½ cup (8 tablespoons) unsalted butter, melted

**FILLING**
4 large eggs
1 cup sugar
⅔ cup fresh lime juice
¼ cup unsalted butter, cut into pieces and softened
1 tablespoon gold tequila

**TOPPING**
1 pint whipping cream
1 tablespoon sugar
1 teaspoon gold tequila

1. To make the crust: Toast the hazelnuts by placing them on a baking sheet in a 350F (180C) oven for 12 minutes. Place the hot nuts in a clean dishtowel and rub together to remove the skins. When cool, grind the nuts by pulsing them very quickly, for a few seconds only, in a food processor.

2. Toast the ground vanilla wafers: Place them on a baking sheet and bake at 350F (180C) for 10 to 15 minutes, until golden brown, stirring once. Leave the oven on.

3. Mix together the vanilla wafers, hazelnuts, coconut, and butter. Press the mixture into a tart pan using your fingers to distribute it evenly on the bottom and sides. Bake for 8 to 10 minutes, until set. Remove from the oven and allow to cool.

4. To make the filling: In a mixing bowl, beat the eggs and sugar with an electric mixer at high speed until the color lightens and the mixture becomes slightly thick. While still mixing, add the lime juice and mix well.

5. Transfer the egg mixture to the top of a double boiler over simmering water. Make sure the bowl is not touching the water. Cook, whisking constantly by hand, until it becomes thick and custardlike. Remove from the heat and whisk in the butter, a piece at a time. Whisk in the tequila.

6. Transfer the mixture to another bowl and cover with plastic wrap pressed against the surface of the custard to prevent a skin from forming. Refrigerate until thoroughly chilled and set. This can be done a day ahead. Do not stir the custard after it is set.

7. To make the topping: Whip the cream with the sugar until stiff peaks form. Beat in the tequila.

8. To assemble the tart: Spoon the custard into the cooled tart shell. Top with the whipped cream. Serve immediately or keep chilled until ready to serve.

# *indian*

■ ■ ■

## *Indian Rice Pudding*

*This aromatic version of rice pudding infuses garam masala, freshly grated nutmeg, cinnamon, and freshly grated orange zest with the creamy comfort of a traditional warm rice pudding. This dish can also be served chilled, but will have a much firmer, set texture. For a super-creamy version, simply add more water or milk toward the end of the cooking process.*

**Preparation Time: 10 minutes** ■ **Cooking Time: 20 to 25 minutes** ■ **Makes 6 servings**

■ ■ ■

2½ cups water

1½ cups half-and-half, fat-free evaporated milk, or plain soy cream

½ teaspoon salt

1 cup jasmine or basmati white rice

1 tablespoon grated orange zest

⅓ cup sugar

¼ teaspoon freshly grated nutmeg

¼ teaspoon ground cinnamon

½ teaspoon Garam Masala (page 120), or purchased

1. Bring water, half-and-half, and salt to a boil.

2. Add rice and orange zest. Reduce heat and boil gently for 15 minutes, uncovered. Check the consistency of the rice; it should be soft.

3. Add the sugar, nutmeg, cinnamon, and Garam Masala and simmer over low heat for 2 to 3 minutes, until the sugar is fully dissolved. The pudding should be soft and slightly soupy.

4. Serve hot.

# BEVERAGES

*Lively Libations*

■ ■ ■

Although I have been dubbed the smoothie queen by friends and family due to my lifelong passion of creating new smoothies for breakfast, I am also a devotee of a good tea or coffee drink.

I have particularly come to appreciate the need for quality ingredients in making drinks of all sorts. My cupboards are filled with some of the finest and most exotic teas from around the world as well as beautiful, freshly roasted organic coffees. But the most important ingredient of all is fresh, clean water.

I couldn't tell you now where I originally heard this tidbit, but one of my friends told me that one should never reuse already-boiled water for coffee or tea. I stand by this as a matter of experience. I always begin with twice-filtered water, once through the house filtering system and again through a water pitcher with a filter. The result is sweet, fresh-tasting water, the best base to a good hot drink.

As for fruit- or milk-based drinks, I have gone organic. Although there are varying qualities of organic products, I feel better using juices and almond, soy, and cow milk that do not contain herbicides, pesticides, insecticides, hormones, or antibiotics. In the best of all worlds, I try to buy fresh, organic produce and juice it when circumstance allows.

We each have to decide for ourselves how much time and money we wish to commit to the quality of the ingredients we use. For me, it's worth it because a beverage is a part of the day's menu. I do not use beverages to wash down food. I drink only water with meals, making the beverages that I do drink a special part of the dining experience. Cheers!

■ ■ ■

■ ■ ■

# *Fresh Ginger Ale*

*This drink serves both as a refreshing libation and as a medicinal, as fresh ginger is commonly used to soothe the stomach and aid in digestion in many indigenous cultures.*

*For a dramatic twist to fresh lemonade, follow this recipe and add the juice of half a lemon.*

**Preparation Time: 10 minutes** ▪ **Cooking Time: 0** ▪ **Makes 1 serving**

■ ■ ■

1½ tablespoons grated fresh ginger

2 tablespoons pure maple syrup

¾ cup carbonated water, such as sparkling water or club soda

1 to 2 teaspoons fresh lime juice (optional)

1. Place the ginger in a small piece of cheesecloth. Squeeze the ginger juice through the cheesecloth into a glass. Discard the ginger, reserving the juice.

2. Add the remaining ingredients. Stir and serve.

# Caye Caulker Smoothie

*This one brings back some exceptionally silly memories. While traveling in Belize, we took the ferry to the small island called Caye Caulker, a place where no cars (and no attitudes) were allowed. After two days, we found ourselves so slow and giddy that we would break into hysterics over, well, over everything. We were laughing so hard at one point that we had to stop and double over. When we straightened up, we found ourselves in front of a little shack that read Susan's Smoothies. Her chilled tropical concoction, served up in old milk bottles, was downright illicit. The following is my take on Susan's smoothies.*

**Preparation Time: 10 minutes** ▪ **Cooking Time: 0** ▪ **Makes 1 serving**

■ ■ ■

> ¾ **cup pineapple juice**
>
> ½ **banana**
>
> ¼ **cup grated fresh coconut (page 232)**
>
> **1 to 1½ tablespoons sweetened condensed milk**
>
> **Generous sprinkling of nutmeg, preferably freshly grated**
>
> **Sprinkling of ground cinnamon**
>
> **2 to 3 ice cubes**

1. Place all the ingredients in a blender. Blend until smooth.

2. Serve immediately.

# Fresh Coconuts

How often have you walked by the homely coconut in the produce aisle without a second glance? This may be because it is not a normal part of our cooking repertoire. However, once a coconut lover takes on a fresh coconut for the first time, a whole new world awaits. The creamy white coconut meat, with just a hint of sweetness, bears no resemblance to store-bought varieties with heavy sweeteners.

Supermarket coconuts are generally found without the smooth, green outer hull. You'll find them stripped down to the hairy brown shell. Choose a coconut that is heavy with coconut juice. You should be able to hear the liquid moving around inside when you shake it.

To remove the milky white flesh from the inside, you will need to punch holes through the two of the three soft "eyes" in the coconut shell. Have a bowl handy to drain the juice into. Once the juice has been drained, take the most substantial hammer you have around the house, along with the coconut, to a solid concrete or brick surface. Sometimes it will take two or three strikes before the coconut will split open. Caution: Do not try to crack open the coconut on the kitchen counter.

Once the coconut is split in half, use a butter knife to pry the meat away from the shell. Avoid using any discolored areas. Carefully peel the brown skin off the white meat with a paring knife. It's best to do this on a cutting board, cutting in a downward motion toward the board to avoid an accident with the knife. You can grate or shred the coconut meat in a food processor or by hand. Each coconut will yield 3 to 4 cups shredded coconut. Place what's not used in a sealable plastic bag. It will keep for about 4 days in the refrigerator and up to 6 months in the freezer.

# Chai

*Chai is commonly found in espresso shops around much of the United States as an alternative to café latte. As a quick alternative to shopping for the spices, you can use Yogi Tea and many other prepackaged chai blends or mixes, which can be found at most natural food stores. The blends contain all the spices called for in this recipe.*

**Preparation Time: 15 minutes ▪ Cooking Time: 8 minutes ▪ Makes 4 servings**

▪ ▪ ▪

Piece of cinnamon stick

Pinch cardamom seeds

3 to 4 whole cloves

3 to 4 black peppercorns

Slice fresh ginger

2 cups filtered water

2 bags black tea

1⅓ cups milk (your choice)

3 to 4 tablespoons honey

Pure vanilla extract, to taste

1. Boil the cinnamon stick, cardamon seeds, cloves, peppercorns, and ginger in the water for 7 to 8 minutes. Remove the pan from the heat, then add the tea bags and let steep for 1 to 2 minutes.

2. Strain out the spices and remove the tea bags. Pour equal amounts of the tea into 4 cups, adding one-quarter of the milk, honey, and vanilla to each cup. Serve hot.

**Variation** Substitute 1½ teaspoons Yogi Tea for the spices.

# *Lassi*

*Lassi is a very refreshing drink to have as a mid-morning or afternoon pick-me-up that not only has a cool, creamy, wonderful flavor, but offers friendly bacteria (from the yogurt) for good intestinal health to nonvegans.*

**Preparation Time: 5 minutes ▪ Cooking Time: 0 ▪ Makes 1 serving**

■ ■ ■

> ⅔ **cup plain yogurt**
> ⅓ **cup sparkling water or milk**
> **Juice of ½ lemon**
> ½ **to 1 tablespoon sugar**
> **2 ice cubes**

1. Briskly stir all ingredients together in a large drinking glass.

2. Serve cold.

# Caffé Cointreau

*The pairing of coffee and orange liqueur is common as an after-dinner drink in parts of Italy.*

**Preparation Time: 5 minutes ▪ Cooking Time: 0 ▪ Makes 1 cup**

▪ ▪ ▪

> 1 cup strong coffee (your favorite)
>
> 2 tablespoons Cointreau
>
> Brown sugar or honey, to taste
>
> 1 small strip fresh orange peel

1. Pour the coffee into a cup and add the Cointreau and brown sugar. Twist the orange peel to release the orange peel oil into the cup. Drop the peel into the coffee.

2. Serve hot.

# Mexican Mocha

*This rich and creamy brew takes on a distinctly different flavor than the American version of café mocha due to the addition of cinnamon, almonds, and vanilla classically found in the cakes of Mexican chocolate or Mexican powdered chocolate. This version is from scratch because it is somewhat difficult to find Mexican chocolate everywhere. Perfect for a cold, winter day!*

**Preparation Time: 10 minutes** ▪ **Cooking Time: 5 minutes** ▪ Makes 1 serving

1 rounded tablespoon sweetened chocolate powder, plus extra for garnish
¼ cup strong coffee
Few drops pure almond extract
Dash of cinnamon
Dash of nutmeg (preferably freshly grated)
¾ cup hot milk

1. Add the chocolate powder to a cup. Pour the coffee over the chocolate and stir until the chocolate is dissolved.

2. Add the almond extract, cinnamon, nutmeg, and hot milk and stir. Garnish with a sprinkling of powdered chocolate.

**Note** For a foamy version, steam the milk with an espresso machine or frother to create a foamy float on the top. Sprinkle the top with powdered chocolate.

# *Turkish Coffee*

*Turkish coffee is not only very strong and sweet, but it is made and served with the grounds in the pot. Allowing a minute or two for the grounds to settle before serving is critical or you will end up with a mouthful of coffee grounds.*

**Preparation Time: 5 minutes** ▪ **Cooking Time: 10 minutes** ▪ **Makes 2 servings**

▪ ▪ ▪

¼ **cup very finely ground coffee**

2 **tablespoons sugar**

1 **cup water**

1. In a very small pot, combine the coffee, sugar, and water. Stir and slowly bring to a simmer. Watch carefully, as you do not want it to come to a rolling boil.

2. When very hot, pour the coffee into demitasse cups. Let it sit for 1 minute to allow the grounds to settle to the bottom of the cup. Serve hot.

# *Doogh*

This refreshing yogurt drink is served after a heavy meal or before bedtime in the Middle East, according to friends from this region. It aids in digestion and helps induce sleep.

**Preparation Time: 10 minutes ▪ Cooking Time: 0 ▪ Makes 1 serving**

½ **cup plain yogurt**
½ **cup seltzer water, chilled**
½ **teaspoon fresh lemon juice**
**Dash of salt**
¼ **teaspoon chopped fresh mint**

1. Combine all the ingredients in a tall glass.

2. Stir and serve.

# Yogurt and Good Health

Yogurt has become one of the biggest food trends of the past two decades, showing up as the base of frozen confections, yogurt-covered peanuts, smoothies, and so on. With all the marketing, the real function of yogurt in the diet has largely been lost. In fact, much of the yogurt you find in commercially prepared foods contains little of the healing properties yogurt is known for.

The beauty of real yogurt lies in the vast number of friendly microorganisms that grow when the milk is exposed to warm temperatures for an extended period of time. The friendly "bugs" are a major player in the flora of our intestinal ecosystem. They are essential for the absorption of nutrients, including vitamins, minerals, and fatty acids; keep unfriendly microbes in check; and support healthy bowel function. When the body is able to absorb and utilize these essential nutrients, the immune system can function more efficiently. It is thought that when the ability to properly absorb nutrients is decreased by an unbalanced intestinal environment, chronic health problems can occur, including some of the most common ailments. The good news is that it is relatively easy to keep levels of the beneficial microorganisms intact by eating yogurt on a regular basis along with plenty of fiber.

Learning to read labels becomes important in determining which yogurt to buy. You want one that contains "living cultures." Many do not. If the yogurt has been frozen, it no longer contains living cultures, as they have been killed in the freezing. One way to ensure you get a living yogurt with a good flavor is to make it yourself. It's surprisingly easy, as most Indian homemakers know. It requires no more than stirring a heaping tablespoon of "living" yogurt into a quart of milk that has been heated to 110F (70C) and allowed to remain at that temperature, covered, for several hours. This not only gives you control over the quality of the yogurt, but also saves money.

## More Yogurt Facts

Yogurt is low in lactose and can often be eaten by those who are lactose intolerant.

It contains calcium, vitamin B-12, and riboflavin, which is important for energy production.

Yogurt is helpful in rebuilding intestinal flora after taking antibiotics.

Yogurt helps combat diarrhea.

Yogurt was developed about 4,000 years ago by Balkan tribes, who needed a way to preserve milk.

### Yogurt in School Lunches

Buy a good-quality plain yogurt with living cultures. Mix in your favorite jam, honey, maple syrup, nuts, or whatever the kids like, into individual containers. When my son was young, I sent him off to school with yogurt mixed with homemade freezer jams almost every day. You can use plastic storage containers or even small canning jars, if the child is older. For fruit yogurts, I like adding homemade freezer jams to avoid additional chemicals and additives found in some of the pre-mixed yogurts.

# *Thai Coffee*

The hallmark of Thai Coffee is its use of sweetened condensed milk, which gives the popular hot or iced coffee drink a sweet and rich flavor. We've chosen to reduce the fat by using nonfat sweetened condensed milk in this recipe without losing any of the flavor.

**Preparation Time: 5 minutes ▪ Cooking Time: 10 minutes ▪ Makes 4 servings**

▪ ▪ ▪

> ½ cup nonfat sweetened condensed milk
>
> 4 cups very strong hot coffee (French roast)

1. This is best served in glass mugs or glasses if you will be serving the coffee iced. In each mug, pour 2 tablespoons condensed milk, being careful not to let it drip on the sides.

2. Turn over a tablespoon and carefully pour the coffee onto the back of the spoon so that it drips into the mug. This will form two layers—one of milk and one of coffee—for a dramatic presentation.

3. Serve hot or iced with a spoon.

# New Orleans Café au Lait

*New Orleans is known for its breakfast treats called beignets, which are served with some New Orleans–style coffee, defined by the blend of coffee beans and chicory. This yields a somewhat smoky-tasting brew with a slight cardamom aftertaste. Here we've smoothed it out by cutting it with hot milk in the French tradition of* au lait *(with milk).*

## Chicory Coffee

Chicory is the secret ingredient in the world-renowned New Orleans café au lait. It is chicory root, which is dried, roasted, and ground like coffee. Chicory adds full body to the coffee without adding caffeine. Some in the natural health field suggest that the bitter chicory is a cleansing fluid used to purify the body, especially in "damp" conditions such as obesity, edema, and candida yeast overgrowth. It can be found in gourmet stores or mail-ordered from one of many Internet sites listed under "chicory coffee."

To make chicory coffee: Place the chicory first, then the coffee grounds in a coffee filter cone (I highly recommend a gold drip filter). Use the drip method of pouring very hot water over the grounds (it is recommended not to overboil the water, as it alters the flavor of the coffee).

**Preparation Time: 5 minutes ▪ Cooking Time: 5 minutes ▪ Makes 1 cup**

▪ ▪ ▪

⅔ **cup frothy hot milk**
⅓ **cup coffee (made with 1 part chicory to 2 parts ground coffee)**
**Sugar, if desired**

1. Pour the hot milk into the coffee and sweeten with sugar according to your preference.

2. Serve hot.

# *Minted Iced Tea*

Hot, sultry Southern afternoons and nights call out for lemon and mint. In our version of minted iced tea, we substitute maple syrup or honey for the white sugar traditionally used. This adds a little complexity to the flavor, and if maple syrup is used, also adds extra vitamins and minerals to this classic refreshment.

**Preparation Time: 15 minutes** ▪ **Cooking Time: 5 minutes** ▪ **Makes 1 quart**

▪ ▪ ▪

　　 2 cups water
　　 1 heaping teaspoon loose black tea
　　 ¼ cup chopped fresh mint leaves
　　 ¼ to ½ cup fresh lemon juice
　　 3 cups ice cubes
　　 Brown sugar, maple syrup, or honey, to taste

1. In a saucepan, bring the water to a boil, then add the tea and mint leaves. Remove from the heat and steep for 10 minutes.

2. Strain the liquid, discarding the tea and mint; add the lemon juice and ice cubes. Chill and serve over ice. Sweeten with brown sugar, maple syrup, or honey, to taste.

## Watermelon-lime Cooler

*I still remember gulping down my first glass of watermelon juice on a hot day while vacationing somewhere in Mexico. Funny, I don't even remember which city I was in, but I remember the taste. I don't think I've felt as refreshed in my life! Since then, watermelon juice has become a staple in the hot months when watermelons are plentiful and inexpensive. And it has a wonderfully cleansing effect on the body when drunk first thing in the morning on an empty stomach. You can eliminate the sugar and lime when you drink it as a morning juice rather than as this mealtime libation.*

**Preparation Time: 10 minutes** ▪ **Cooking Time: 0** ▪ **Makes 1 serving**

▪ ▪ ▪

**2-inch thick slice of watermelon, rind and seeds removed**
**1 tablespoon fresh lime juice**
**2 tablespoons simple syrup (see Note below)**
**Ice cubes**

1. Place the watermelon in a blender and puree until it becomes a smooth liquid.

2. Strain through a fine-mesh sieve or cheesecloth-lined strainer. Push on the pulp with a butter knife to make sure you get all the juice out.

3. Add the lime juice and simple syrup and stir. Serve over ice.

**Note:** Simple syrup is made by combining equal portions of sugar and water and heating them until the sugar has dissolved. This can be used to sweeten the base of any drink, hot or cold.

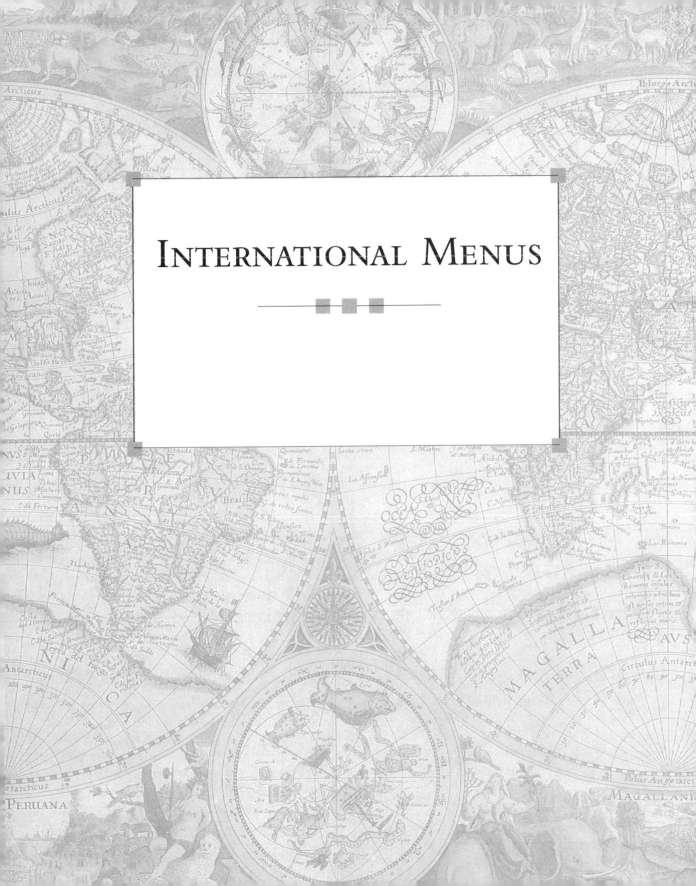

# INTERNATIONAL MENUS

■ ■ ■

I'll never forget my first meal on the island of Jamaica. It wasn't just the food but the feeling of this lush, verdant tropical world of rhythm and spice. We were on an old plantation that was supporting a restaurant in its newest incarnation. The sides of the restaurant were open to the elements, exposing as lush a view as I had seen—thick, bright-green foliage, tropical flowers, and birds. The inside décor reflected the natural environment—mats made from native grasses, wooden plates, dark hardwood beams, and living plants of all kinds.

I ordered the fruit plate with homemade date nut bread and lime sherbet. Though I was raised in California and exposed to an abundance of fresh fruit my entire life, what lay before me was of a different order of magnitude on the taste scale. The sweet, topical fruits had been freshly picked, not flown in. Melons melted in my mouth, the pineapple was bursting with sweet juice, mangos were both tart and sweet on the tongue, and all were cooled off with a snowy melt of lime sherbet.

Like most visitors, we were there for the beautiful, white beaches and aqua-blue water, but it was the lush, fertile interior that captivated me, as it did those to first reach the Caribbean shores. This is evidenced in some of the original names of the islands: Dominica's name in Caribs is "Tall Is Her Body," Martinique was known in Taino as "Flower Island," and Montserrat was originally "Land of the Prickly Pear."

Life in the Caribbean is as sweet as her fruits, with the sounds of calypso, conga, and rhumba filling the air. These rhythms are deeply rooted in both African and Spanish music, two of the major influences in the cuisine. From dishes with native jerk spices to sweet potatoes with cloves to tropical coconut drinks and the flavors of ginger and lime brightening an array of dishes, Caribbean cuisine is one of the most difficult to categorize. Simply put, whoever landed on one of her shores took one look, declared it home, and began cooking up what they knew, using everything the islands produced and planting the rest.

The most intoxicating of all the island's treasures, however, is the laughter. Deep, rich, belly laughs are everywhere. Yes, the island's laughter bounces through my heart and soul as I commit these memories to paper.

# China

It is a common Buddhist practice to pause before the first bite of a meal, contemplating all the people and all the work that brought the food to the table. It's this reverence for the land, in this nation of gardeners and farmers, that permeates the dining experience. From the industrial agricultural plains to small truck gardens, it is a sin in the eyes of one who works the land to leave a grain of rice in your bowl at the end of the meal. From this sacred space, a quiet and respectful ritual was born. Food is to be savored, not gobbled up. Chopsticks move the delicately sliced vegetables to the mouth deftly, without noise.

Another aspect of the Chinese dining ritual is that no one leaves hungry. This was brought to my attention by a friend who was born and raised in Peking. When the two of us would go out for Chinese food, I would witness an act of eating unparalleled in my experience. Knowing that I generally have a small evening meal, my friend would proceed to order enough food for six, including her favorite, a piece of roasted pork weighing about 1½ to 2 pounds. I am certain that my mouth was agape the first time I witnessed her eat the entire bounty on the table, save for a few pea shoots. I came to understand that she treated these dining experiences as a banquet, which the Chinese revere. These grand and ritualistic meals could last for several days in ancient times, with guests sleeping beside the table between courses.

For a more spare dining experience, there is dim sum. Here, small amounts of food can be ordered dish by dish. One of the most popular dim sum dishes is mu shu crepes (a vegetarian version is on page 96). In general, Chinese cuisine lends itself to the vegetarian diet, as a vast array of dishes are made from a base of mushrooms, tofu, eggs, rice, noodles, vegetables, and vegetable broth.

The cuisine in this vast land is as varied as the geography itself, with food from the Szechwan (or "Four Rivers") garlicky and spicy, the Cantonese filled with bean sauce and broths, and mild Mandarin cuisine featuring sesame oil and soybean paste. The following menu contains a suggestion of each.

**GREEN ONION PANCAKES   3**

**CHINESE RAVIOLIS IN VEGETABLE BROTH   70**

**MU SHU VEGETABLES   96**

**EGG FOO YONG   99**

**CANDIED GINGER COOKIES   200**

**OOLONG TEA**

*When eating bamboo sprouts, remember the hand that planted them.*
**—Buddha**

*No matter what kind of hardship is faced in life—one is one's own master on one's own stove.*
—*Russian proverb*

Eastern Europe is a big place, with harsh weather and eternally changing boundaries. It includes Russia, the Ukraine, Belarus, Estonia, Latvia, Lithuania, Poland, Hungary, the Czech Republic, Slovakia, Bulgaria, and Romania—hundreds of thousands of square miles swept by icy drifts of snow in the winter and humid heat in the summer. It's a place that begs for comfort and solace and earthy, pungent dishes that stick to the ribs. Garlic, onions, horseradish, beets, potatoes, and other cold-weather vegetables are the principal players in a region known for its hearty comfort foods.

A typical meal would begin with a bowl of soup, which I found to mean borscht. If I may digress, years ago, my mother was traveling in the former Soviet Union with a group from California. In her continued attempts to heal the world, she arrived laden with gifts of Levi's, designer tennis shoes, audio cassettes, and lapel buttons that read "Let's Be Friends" in both English and Russian. Baffled when the Moscovites cast a suspicious glance at her attempts to distribute the buttons, Mom was joyful to find a friendly reaction in Henri. Henri was a 17-year-old boy who fully appreciated her gesture of friendship (especially the tennis shoes and audio cassettes!) whom she met at the Intercontinental Hotel where he and his mother, Maria, were enjoying a Mother's Day lunch. Eye contact was made. Well acquainted with the black market, Henri understood and initiated contact with my mother in a time when that was a risky endeavor. My father, who was sleeping, awakened with a jolt, surprised to see the gangly teen Mom had brought to the room. She opened her suitcase of gifts for Henri, and a lasting friendship was born. They wrote and sent each other desirable objects from their respective countries. After much red tape, a trip was arranged for Henri and his mother to visit the United States.

On their first day out, we took them to a restaurant that had an extensive menu. Although Maria had been an English teacher all her life, the choices proved to be overwhelming. She glanced at the menu, then quietly closed it and placed it on the table. When asked for her order she simply said, "Soup." The waiter asked, "Which soup?" Maria was surprised. She only knew one kind of soup, borscht.

Knowing the importance of soup at the Eastern European table, I included my dear deceased Russian friend, Madame Bovie's, constantly changing versions of borscht as part of this menu.

# France

France is where I fell in love with food. I mean, *really* fell in love. Being one who enjoys the daily food-shopping ritual, I was right in stride with the other women at the market, picking through the day's crop of tomatoes, peaches, or plums. I would even follow them into the *supermarche* to see what kind of wines they bought for the nightly table. The cheese merchants were my favorites, as they offered me little wedges from the pungent golden- and cream-colored wheels. But perhaps the best experience of all was being out with friends late at night as the first *pain au chocolat* (chocolate-filled croissant) was removed from the boulangerie oven. The thought nearly sends me to the closest French bakery!

Many years have passed since that first contact with the delights of the French table, and I have since taken my son, Stuart, to discover these joys for himself. His first love at first bite? What else? *Pain au chocolat!* And while man cannot live by bread alone, he would swear you could come pretty close to doing so in France.

But by no means is having to eat your vegetables a punishment when contrasted to *pain au chocolat*. The French are masters at taking simple ingredients and making them sublime, especially vegetables. With just a touch of olive oil, a pinch of herbs, and a dash of sea salt, the humblest of earth's produce is turned into a gourmet's delight. And with a barnyard or garden just a hop away from the city center, there is no shortage of vegetables from which to choose. In truth, it's the simple meal, shared in the homes of friends, that is at the heart of French cuisine, not the sauce-laden haute cuisine of old, meals made with tomatoes that are picked fresh from the garden along with a handful of herbs from the dry southern French terrain. As soon as the first glass of pastis disappears, a delectable thin crust pizza appears from the host's oven, someone brings out a guitar, and the languages merge as we (badly) sing some famous tune. Fresh green lettuce dressed with Dijon, olive oil, and balsamic vinegar arrives with a crusty loaf of bread and wine, followed by cheese and fruit plates and finally a tart and coffee. It's the beauty of this simple fare that captivates the hearts of those who have long-standing love affairs with France.

**ONION TART   9**

**WILD MUSHROOM SOUP WITH CRÈME FRAÎCHE   74**

**TENDER GREENS WITH PROVENÇAL DRESSING   45**

**PROVENÇAL POTATO GRATIN   175**

**APPLE AND SESAME TART TATIN   204**

**CAFÉ AU LAIT**

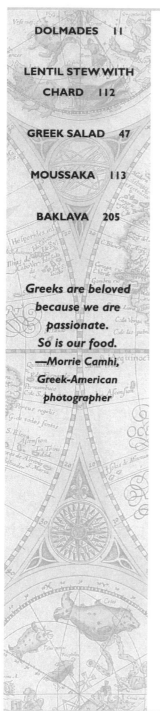

*Greeks are beloved because we are passionate. So is our food.*
—*Morrie Camhi, Greek-American photographer*

Did you know that Pythagoras was a vegetarian and that Plutarch was as well? Why not? This sun-drenched land offers up some of the most marvelous flavors on earth: piquant dry black olives, rich green olive oils, grapes, pine nuts, walnuts, goat cheeses, lemons, melons, and a plethora of spices and herbs. Roasted eggplant and fresh garlic pureed into dips are lustily mopped up with pieces of pita bread. All of this is part of a dining tradition that dates back more than 2,000 years.

The value of good food was understood far beyond its culinary contribution. The great thinkers of the day viewed the native foods and seasonings as much a medicine as a pleasure. In 400 B.C., Hippocrates wrote numerous treatises on the medicinal role of plants such as saffron, cinnamon, thyme, coriander, mint, and marjoram. Today, researchers are crediting the olive oil-, vegetable- and legume-rich diet as a decidedly healthful way to live. Health aside, its simply splendid fare!

Having spent only brief times in Greece, most of my experiences with Greek cuisine have come in the form of celebrations—weddings, holidays, birthdays, recitals—it seems there is no shortage of reasons for celebrations among my Greek friends and acquaintances. The table always overflows with the earthy and pungent dishes—dolmades, moussaka, lentils and favas swimming in tomato sauce and olive oil, and hummus. Teasing and laughter accompany each mouthful. Music swirls through the room. These get-togethers are truly sensual and passionate affairs.

The event is wrapped up with thick Greek coffee, in the style of To Cafenio, the coffeehouses spotted across the cities and villages, offering sticky desserts sweet with honey to accompany the afternoon's pungent brew. It's here, over a cup of coffee, that mid-afternoon acquaintances become lifelong friends.

# India

It is called Mother India for good reason. This ancient land with seventeen formally recognized languages is a study in multiplicity of culture, experience, spiritual belief, race, creed, and cuisine. India is a nation of nations that accommodates a vast array of experience and heritage and still somehow remains a country. The scale of the place is hard to comprehend; it is a country of subcontinent proportions. Because of its vastness, there is actually no national cuisine, but selections of regional dishes from throughout the country, though it might seem otherwise to one who knows India only through the neighborhood Indian restaurant.

The cuisine most people from my home region of Northern California are familiar with is from the northern Punjab region, which is the breadbasket of India, similar to the Central Valley of California. Because of this close association with the land, many more people from the Punjab have settled in Northern California than natives of Southern India. When traveling around the United States, however, you will see the influence of many regions in the Indian cuisine. The dishes in this menu are mostly influenced by Punjabi fare because I learned how to prepare Indian cuisine from Mrs. Nirmal Dhinsa, the mother of my friend Monica.

Mrs. Dhinsa's cuisine is renowned in the central California city they now call home. Spicy potato-filled pastries called *samosas* are often the first item on the table, followed by *dahl* curried vegetables and legumes, rice, spicy creamed spinach, and yogurt. The sumptuous feasts are followed by chai and sweet rice puddings.

As the years have passed, Monica and I have both become so busy with our respective lives that dinners are infrequent. This has left me with no choice but to cook the spicy and aromatic cuisine myself. But I admit, I would still rather be sitting at the Dhinsas' table, enjoying the kind and soft conversation with her lovely family while feasting on some of the best Indian cuisine I have ever tasted.

Most of the spices we have come to think of as universal—ginger, turmeric, nutmeg, clove, vanilla, cinnamon, mustard, aniseed, cumin, dill, celery seed, and even pepper—are all grown in India. The thousands of years old business of growing and trading spices to the rest of the world currently brings more than $350 million a year to India's coffers. So it should not be surprising to find the heavy use of spice as the one common denominator to all Indian cuisine.

BAKED SAMOSAS   15

CURRIED
CAULIFLOWER SOUP
76

INDIA HOUSE
FRITTATA   111

RAITA   48

INDIAN RICE PUDDING
226

CHAI   233

It had been a long, drizzly day, pushing through the crowded streets of Florence, Italy, and my feet were about to give out after a day of searching for Italian cotton and silk. As luck would have it, I was standing in front of one of the city's most popular Tuscan restaurants. One peek in the window and I knew I would go no farther. Waiters in black and white were hustling steaming plates of pasta to the hungry patrons, and a line was beginning to form behind me.

The first thing an uninitiated American in Italy would notice is the spartan appearance of the pasta dishes. The noodles are not smothered in sauces, as is often the case in "traditional" Italian restaurants in the United States. Rather, they may come with as little as chopped garlic, olive oil, and shaved Parmesan. An alfredo sauce could be just a couple tablespoons of cream added to the above. And of course, olive oil is at the center of each table. Patrons drizzle or drop one golden tear of oil at a time onto their salads, soups, pasta, rice—whatever they wish.

Throughout Italy you will find the same minimalist approaches to dining. In fact, you're required to pay a "cover charge" at some *trattorias* for the cost of the bread and oil, as well as the cleaning of the tablecloth. And presentation of the food is not a priority. It's served the way a busy mother would serve you. But once the garlic, tomatoes, basil, and olive oil reach your nose, you're as comforted as if you were wrapped in your mother's arms. With a Chianti or Brunello di Montalcino to soften the senses, a feeling of total contentment spreads throughout.

Soon it's time to wind your way home, and an espresso is in order. There will be the inevitable mark of the perfect cup, the *crema,* or caramel-colored froth that floats on the surface of the chocolate-colored brew. A cappuccino offers some of the sweetest and freshest-tasting milk you've ever experienced. Love abounds! That's because Italians know about love. They love their families, their lovers, their land, and of course, their food. You can almost feel a cumulative heartbeat in each and every city and village you enter.

# Japan

In Japan, the curious and beautiful relationship of nature and formality are on every plate and in every bowl. Just walk by any restaurant window to see plastic replicas of sushi, noodles, rice, and soups arranged in ceremonial patterns on dark lacquer trays. A visual menu, these displays also reveal the Japanese cultural values of grace and order. Anyone can order sushi by simply pointing. It is a visual practice that leads to a more peaceful dining experience. Dining in Japan is calm; the courses are sequential and structured. First, miso soup, then pickled greens, followed by main courses that may be broiled, grilled, pan-fried, or stir-fried. Rice is served toward the end—sticky, not fluffy. The meal may be closed with a simple plate of sliced orange wedges and more green tea.

Even today, as life in Japan moves at breathtaking speeds, it is an honor to cook for someone and an honor to be invited for a meal. Friends pour tea for each other, never for themselves. Meals are arranged artfully and with care, though the food itself may be simple by Western standards. The freshest ingredients available can be costly but are an integral part of the well-done meal in Japan.

At the heart of the Japanese diet is soy in the form of tofu, shoyu (soy sauce), raw beans, and a salted bean paste known as miso. Although families are generally too busy to make their own miso anymore, each region has a distinctive way of preparing miso soup, the Japanese equivalent of chicken noodle soup. Miso has a remarkable ability to comfort the body and mind as well as boost the immune system. Part of this is the warmth and mild and salty flavor along with healthful enzymes. But miso has other important properties that contribute to good health, which is why a bowl is promptly placed in front of the infirmed once food can be taken again.

The emphasis on both health and pleasure is seen throughout the Japanese diet. Naturally low in fat, the cuisine is heavy on colorful vegetables, vegetable and fish broths (we focus on vegetable bases), rice, and buckwheat noodles. Dishes are made to sparkle with ginger, rice vinegar, sesame oil, shoyu sauce, and sugar. Color dominates the serving plate, as a meal is prepared as much for the eye as the palate. Place settings are natural and graceful with different ceramic dishware for the changing seasons and special occasions. The ultimate beauty of the Japanese table setting is its reflection of the surrounding environment, the sand, sky, sea, and forests.

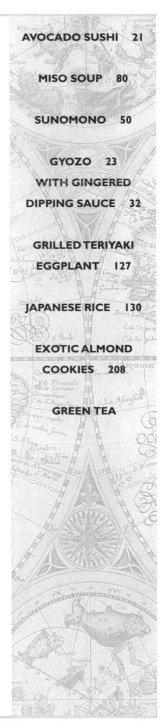

**AVOCADO SUSHI   21**

**MISO SOUP   80**

**SUNOMONO   50**

**GYOZO   23
WITH GINGERED
DIPPING SAUCE   32**

**GRILLED TERIYAKI
EGGPLANT   127**

**JAPANESE RICE   130**

**EXOTIC ALMOND
COOKIES   208**

**GREEN TEA**

A smile immediately comes to my face at the thought of my time spent in Mexico. Time there seems to pass differently—slower, happier. It's as though Mexico's people have found some way to deal with life that shields the heart from the damage of the world's harshness. A strong family tradition, religion, and the comfort of the native foods would likely all play a part in the force behind the slow, easy smiles I've encountered.

When I refer to comfort foods, comfort is spelled with a capital C in Mexico. One of the most popular dishes, tacos, starts with the soul of Mexican cuisine, the tortilla. Tortilla-making is often a social event. The women of the town gather and pat the round balls of either corn or flour dough into the familiar shape while exchanging news and gossip of the day. This is a communal and lively experience with children playing underfoot. Back at home the tortillas are transformed into tacos, chips, flautas, enchiladas, tostadas, and chilaquiles. Spicy, filling, and hot, all are satisfying to the body and soul.

Tortillas are only one use of masa, a finely ground cornmeal. Masa is also used to make tamales and even cakes and puddings. The uses are as varied as the land itself. Mexico possesses mountains and highlands, lowlands, steamy rainforests, jungles, and coastal beauty with open-air homes where people live casually and naturally. Even in the poorest regions, you see a pride in the simple tasks. I'm reminded of seeing a women with a simple home and barren yard sweeping the earth outside, removing any stray bits of debris that may have landed in her yard, smiling as she swept.

Having grown up with Mexican food in California, I find this is often one of the most comfortable types of cuisine for new vegetarians to relate to, as the Mexican diet is rich in meatless ingredients. Corn, rice, beans, vegetables, chiles, and hot and pungent spices are the basis of many Mexican dishes. Citrus fruits, especially lemon and lime, add sparkle to the fresher and lighter dishes. A wide array of tropical fruits like mango, jicama, papaya, and berries sweeten up the menu. But none of the above is sweeter than a gentle hand sharing the day's culinary offerings with a passing friend or even a stranger.

# Middle East

I cannot think of Middle Eastern food without thinking of the women who, in awe, I dubbed "the Persian Kittens." So sensual were their lives, as I imagined it, that they inspired me to learn to prepare their cuisine to somehow feel closer to their life experience.

They all had proper educations; perfect bodies; smooth, golden skin; beautifully cut clothing; an abundance of fine jewelry; thick and luxurious hair; and wealthy husbands. They brought with them from Iran all their womanly skills and wiles, including the art of cooking. There were regular parties, with the hostess making all the food for her soirees, spending days in the kitchen to ensure the sauces were just right, the rice fluffy, and the desserts sumptuous. And after dinner came the dancing, usually women with women as the men watched. I was mesmerized to see a sinuous and sensual, downright steamy, form of movement I thought belonged only to old movies with dramatically lit black-and-white scenes, where a Caucasian, blue-eyed woman with artificially darkened skin would play the love object of a handsome sheik in his ceremonial Bedouin tent.

Much to my good fortune, one of the women taught me some of her favorite family recipes. I found the cuisine to be colorful, aromatic, earthy, and rich. Not rich as in laden with fat, but rich as in the density of the food. The arid golden-colored terrain offers foods that do not require large amounts of water—nuts, figs, dates, seeds, spices and herbs, grapes, legumes, and potatoes. I found the most outstanding feature of the cuisine to be the abundant use of herbs. A Middle Eastern omelet contains only enough egg to bind a bounty of fresh green herbs such as dill, parsley, and chives laced with fennel seed, turmeric, nutmeg, and chopped nuts.

Adding to the healthful properties of the Middle Eastern diet is the liberal consumption of yogurt. Yogurt is used at the base of sauces, served with fruit, eaten plain, and is the base of a popular drink called Doogh (page 238). But the sensual pleasures are not sacrificed, as a meal is finished with thick Turkish coffee and a small dessert.

# Southeast Asia

This part of the world makes one feel as though time is standing still. Hands still work the verdant land. The price of daily rations fluctuates by the transaction, skyrocketing when doing business with a foreigner. Life for many is basic, the cuisine direct and aromatic.

My first contact with Southeast Asia was at the tail end of the Vietnam War. Beauty and sorrow were woven together everywhere the eye turned. Beautiful young women, holding onto new babies, cried softly and waved a final good-bye as their American soldier boyfriends boarded military aircraft bound for their U.S. homes and lives. The young men cried, too. Villagers lived in dwellings strung between trees, with the entire family in one room. A pot of fish soup would send steam up into the street. Lobster dinners were two dollars and silk a dollar a yard. The Southeast Asia I knew still exists today in many of the villages, although the cities have become decidedly more modern. But one only needs to take a look back to understand the underlying capabilities of the culture.

The countries of Vietnam and Thailand are steeped in antiquity, with its people living along the waterways for nearly 10,000 years. The Thai people taught the Vietnamese how to cultivate the land and harness the monsoons for the growing of rice. They did this by building a system of dykes that precedes written history.

In spite of the farming economy and lifestyle, the heritage of this region is sophisticated and intellectual. Poetry, music, painting, and other arts flourished here long before Europe was settled. Friendships forged through early trade between Siam, Indonesia, Persia, and countries of the Mediterranean had a dominant influence on the evolution of the cuisine. The resulting dining traditions have been well preserved, with recipes being handed down from generation to generation in each region.

Because of the number of Buddhists, vegetarianism is a more common way of life here than in most other countries. And the fertile soil supports an abundance of fresh vegetables and herbs. The cuisine is fresh and crunchy, seasoned with green curries, lemongrass, galanga, hot chilies, and hoisin sauce. These dishes are so flavorful, fresh, and healthful that Southeast Asian cuisine is rapidly becoming among the most popular fare in the restaurant industry.

# Coastal Fresh

The new cuisine in the United States has been greatly affected by the coastal influence. Whether in the Great Northwest, on the California coast, or on the Eastern Seaboard, there is a freedom and a sense of daring, where anything seems possible both in real life and the world of cuisine.

Having been raised in Northern California, I grew up with the luxury of a year-round supply of fresh produce. While most of the world has had the pleasure of plump, succulent seasonal fruits and vegetables, the sheer variety of produce available at a plethora of outdoor farmers' markets and supermarkets available year-round can be mind-boggling in milder climates. When you couple this perpetual supply of quality ingredients with the propensity for risk-taking and free expression that is often found in the coastal metropolitan areas, you have an explosive dynamic on the food scene, at times to a fault.

I have had the pleasure of dining at some of the best restaurants along the coasts, as well as spending time with a good number of the top chefs, and although I have tasted many truly ingenious culinary masterpieces, the creativity sometimes goes over the top. This happens when one is stretching for "unique." Pairing odd combinations of foods, herbs, and spices is tricky and often backfires. This is when I begin looking back to the classics of other cuisine for influences, such as the simplicity of southern French and Italian cuisine. When looking to the freshness and quality of ingredients as the primary flavor source in a recipe, you seldom go wrong.

Fortunately, the culinary playing field has been leveled around the country with a restaurant in Chicago or St. Louis having access to much of the same fine produce as the coastal regions. And in truth, the chefs who have made the new cuisine popular often move from city to city. Coastal Fresh really has more to do with the adventurous spirit of creativity combined with availability of fine, fresh produce, no matter where the cuisine is prepared.

**GRILLED EGGPLANT DIP  34**

**GARDEN PESTO SOUP WITH PINE NUTS  84**

**QUINOA AND WILD RICE SALAD WITH DRIED APRICOTS  56**

**RED PEPPER RAVIOLI  146**

**LEMON CHEESECAKE WITH GINGERSNAP CRUST  217**

# Cajun-Creole

They came by boat, by foot, by coach; they came from France, Spain, Italy, Canada, Africa, the Caribbean, and finally Germany. All of these settlers were preceded by Native Americans, and it was the Native American contribution of native-grown spices that played a central role in the development of the cuisine from this "Crescent City" that lies at the crook of the Mississippi River. Is it a wonder that it's difficult to give a quick description of Cajun and Creole cuisine?

Perhaps the most distinct spice the Choctaws brought to the marketplace was filé, ground dried sassafras leaves, for gumbo. The Spanish brought their tradition of paella, a curried rice and shellfish dish, which soon evolved into jambalaya, the classic one-pot dinner. Veterans of the Mexican-American war brought the hot chilies that heat up Cajun cuisine in the form of seeds from Mexico. Clearly, every meal was a voyage that brought together the tastes and smells of much of the known world.

Now, the word *vegetarian* is not the first word to pop to mind when conjuring up visions of cuisine of the bayou. Before my vegetarian days, I was sitting at a festive dinner in Baton Rouge next to a Creole octogenarian who had just finished singing the French national anthem before forks and knives were raised. The man instructed me on the proper way in which to consume the steaming pile of crawfish lying in front of me on the paper-covered table. It seems the pearls of the feast were the entrails of the crawfish, which were to be scooped out with the back of the thumbnail and eaten. I believe this experience was instrumental in my decision to become a vegetarian!

Nevertheless, the intoxicating smells of gumbo, red beans and rice, and jambalaya called, and once you adjust your ingredient list a bit, these dishes can be very satisfying without the sausage and ham hocks. In fact, gardens enriched by yearly flooding of the wetlands and swamp regions grow an abundance of vegetables such as okra, root vegetables, and greens, which have historically provided the bulk for the pungent and spicy cuisine.

With this homey fare comes the gracious hospitality of the South. No better example is the one-pot gumbos and jambalaya, which lends itself to expansion of the guest list at a moment's notice. As a prominent belle of New Orleans once said, "There is always enough food among friends."

# New Southern

*Languid, sensual,* and *secretive* are the first words that come to mind when I think of time spent in the South. This ripe, bucolic land has given birth to every kind of crop and human experience throughout its fascinating and turbulent history. It's no surprise that the cuisine here is oriented toward grace and comfort—steaming bowls of grits, potatoes and gravy, cobblers, and creamed greens. Here, lemonade and refreshing sweet teas are still served on porches.

Perhaps the most sensual day of my life was spent on the banks of the Chattahoochee River in the outskirts of Atlanta. A friend and I had been invited to a luncheon being given by a true Southern belle. She had been raised with little white gloves and debutante balls, and had learned well the art of Southern hospitality.

Our hostess escorted us to a table set up in the backyard on the riverbank. In the fourth place, as there were only three of us, was a horn-of-plenty with fresh summer fruits spilling generously onto the table. Wine and little sandwiches were served, all the while a warm and slightly humid breeze was circling around our arms, faces, and ankles under the table. After lunch, warmed by the afternoon, fruit, and wine, our hostess's husband pulled up to the bank in a river barge he had acquired. We hopped onboard and drifted down the Chattahoochee. The sky darkened with thunderclouds as we passed under the large, sweeping branches of tulip poplars, maples, pines, and water oaks.

As for its cuisine, the New South has grown beyond the heavy meals of the past and embraced a lighter style of cuisine, while surrendering none of the flavor. Because smoked pork is a traditional seasoning in this region, I've incorporated the use of hickory-smoked tofu into the following menu with a surprisingly good result. Grits paired with smoky Cheddar give all the comfort of the South. And we finish the meal with, if I may say so, one of the best bread puddings anywhere. If you choose to go lighter, a fresh lemon sorbet in lemon peel cups is also included. The point here is that you do not have to give up all your favorite foods just because you've decided to lighten your diet. We can all still use a little comfort from time to time.

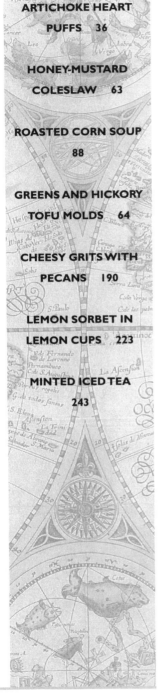

**ARTICHOKE HEART PUFFS  36**

**HONEY-MUSTARD COLESLAW  63**

**ROASTED CORN SOUP  88**

**GREENS AND HICKORY TOFU MOLDS  64**

**CHEESY GRITS WITH PECANS  190**

**LEMON SORBET IN LEMON CUPS  223**

**MINTED ICED TEA  243**

There's an isolation and sense of mystery that pervades the arid, dramatic landscape of the southwestern states of Arizona and New Mexico. It's this mystique that captivated the celebrated artist Georgia O'Keeffe when she stated "I have these things in my head that are not like anything anyone has taught me." Her art reflects this quietude with lush, singular, organic objects that pull from the warmth of the terrain.

The casual climate is noticeable in every aspect of Southwestern life. Rarely will you see a man in a tie, nor a woman in heels, save for an avant garde art opening at a Santa Fe or Sedona gallery. And the cuisine is as unfussy as the lifestyle, a reflection of the hot, earthy, and piquant land. The influences of its roots are visible everywhere; in the pueblo style architecture where soft and softer browns blend with the earth and the beautiful red-and-black hand-tied rugs and strands of firey red chilies braided together. This cuisine is a marriage between that of the early Native American habitants and Hispanic settlers, the base ingredients common to both cultures—beans, rice, corn, squash, and chilies.

This is where chilies thrive, and any local will tell you that they grow the best chilies in the world. Chili production in the Southwest centers on Hatch, New Mexico (see page 135), but chili fields can also be found throughout Texas and Arizona. Chiles are found in just about everything here, not the least of which is steaming hot bowls of chili. Good-natured arguments frequently pop up over whether green or red chilies are best. When dining at a Tex-Mex or Southwest-style restaurant, it's always a good idea to ask which is the hottest. I should share with you that you might not always be given useful information here. I asked this question before ordering my first bowl of chili at a popular Santa Fe diner. The waitress, a native of the region, suggested I might enjoy the green chili more. I saw a slow smirk spread across her face as I took my first spoonful. I suppose it was some kind of initiation. Beads of sweat rolling down my forehead, my mouth on fire, I ordered a glass of ice water and ice cream to bring my senses back to normal. I couldn't tell you if it tasted good or bad, just hot!

# Metric Conversion Charts

| Comparison to Metric Measure | | | | |
|---|---|---|---|---|
| **When You Know** | **Symbol** | **Multiply By** | **To Find** | **Symbol** |
| teaspoons | tsp | 5.0 | milliliters | ml |
| tablespoons | tbsp | 15.0 | milliliters | ml |
| fluid ounces | fl. oz. | 30.0 | milliliters | ml |
| cups | c | 0.24 | liters | l |
| pints | pt. | 0.47 | liters | l |
| quarts | qt. | 0.95 | liters | l |
| ounces | oz. | 28.0 | grams | g |
| pounds | lb. | 0.45 | kilograms | kg |
| Fahrenheit | F | 5/9 (after subtracting 32) | Celsius | C |

| Fahrenheit to Celsius | |
|---|---|
| **F** | **C** |
| 200–205 | 95 |
| 229–225 | 105 |
| 245–250 | 120 |
| 275 | 135 |
| 300–305 | 150 |
| 325–330 | 165 |
| 345–350 | 175 |
| 370–375 | 190 |
| 400–405 | 205 |
| 425–430 | 220 |
| 445–450 | 230 |
| 470–475 | 245 |
| 500 | 260 |

| Liquid Measure to Liters | | |
|---|---|---|
| 1/4 cup | = | 0.06 liters |
| 1/2 cup | = | 0.12 liters |
| 3/4 cup | = | 0.18 liters |
| 1 cup | = | 0.24 liters |
| 1 1/4 cups | = | 0.30 liters |
| 1 1/2 cups | = | 0.36 liters |
| 2 cups | = | 0.48 liters |
| 2 1/2 cups | = | 0.60 liters |
| 3 cups | = | 0.72 liters |
| 3 1/2 cups | = | 0.84 liters |
| 4 cups | = | 0.96 liters |
| 4 1/2 cups | = | 1.08 liters |
| 5 cups | = | 1.20 liters |
| 5 1/2 cups | = | 1.32 liters |

| Liquid Measure to Milliliters | | |
|---|---|---|
| 1/4 teaspoon | = | 1.25 milliliters |
| 1/2 teaspoon | = | 2.50 milliliters |
| 3/4 teaspoon | = | 3.75 milliliters |
| 1 teaspoon | = | 5.00 milliliters |
| 1 1/4 teaspoons | = | 6.25 milliliters |
| 1 1/2 teaspoons | = | 7.50 milliliters |
| 1 3/4 teaspoons | = | 8.75 milliliters |
| 2 teaspoons | = | 10.0 milliliters |
| 1 tablespoon | = | 15.0 milliliters |
| 2 tablespoons | = | 30.0 milliliters |

# INDEX